WE'RE ALIVE AND LIFE GOES ON

"And one last time we seized each other's image, for life and for death . . . for eternity."

—from *Catherine Will Become a Soldier*
by Adrianne Thomas

WE'RE ALIVE
AND LIFE GOES ON

A THERESIENSTADT DIARY

EVA ROUBÍČKOVÁ

Translated by ZAIA ALEXANDER

Foreword by VIRGINIA EUWER WOLFF

Henry Holt and Company ■ New York

I would like to express my gratitude to Michael Heim, who has been a guiding force throughout the translation. I also thank Eva Roubíčková and her daughter Vera Wiser for their generosity and patience in helping me to resurrect worlds and concepts that would otherwise have been untranslatable.

—Zaia Alexander

Henry Holt and Company, Inc.

Publishers since 1866

115 West 18th Street

New York, New York 10011

Henry Holt is a registered
trademark of Henry Holt and Company, Inc.
Copyright © 1998 by Eva Mändlová Roubíčková
All rights reserved.
Published in Canada by Fitzhenry & Whiteside Ltd.,
195 Allstate Parkway, Markham, Ontario L3R 4T8.

Library of Congress Cataloging-in-Publication Data
Roubíčková, Eva Mändlová.
We're alive and life goes on: Theresienstadt diary / by Eva
Mändlová Roubíčková; translated by Zaia Alexander; foreword by
Virginia Euwer Wolff.
p.   cm.
Summary: Presents the diary entries of a young woman living in the
Jewish ghetto of Theresienstadt, a model concentration camp designed
by the Nazis to show to the Red Cross and other humanitarian
organizations.
1. Roubíčková, Eva Mändlová—Diaries.   2. Holocaust, Jewish
(1939–1945)—Czechoslovakia—Personal narratives.   3. Jews—
Persecutions—Czechoslovakia.   4. Theresienstadt (Concentration
camp).   5. Czechoslovakia—Ethnic relations.   I. Alexander, Zaia.
II. Wolff, Virginia Euwer.   III. Title.
DS135.C97R68   1998   940.53′18′09437—dc21   97-18576

ISBN 0-8050-5352-2
First Edition—1998
Printed in the United States of America on acid-free paper. ∞
1 3 5 7 9 10 8 6 4 2

To Richard

CONTENTS

FOREWORD

HOW TO TELL the monstrous story of Hitler to the world? Sometimes it begins with a potato. Or a pair of shoes. Small things
take on enormous importance as we try to understand the
horrifying scope and depth of the Nazi poison.

Eva Roubíčková, a privileged young girl in Bohemia, wore
pretty dresses, loved tennis and skiing, went to school, fell in
love. Her crime was that she was Jewish.

Suddenly in 1941, her life turned sideways. She was sent by
train to Theresienstadt, a camp where Jews were held prisoner
in a mystifying limbo, not knowing when or even whether they
would be "sent to Poland." Nor did they have any real idea of
what these one-way "transports to Poland" meant.

They had no way of knowing that they were part of what
would later be called the Holocaust.

Theresienstadt prisoners didn't have their heads shaved;
they had bathrooms and beds and work assignments. But they
lived with rigid rules and imprisonment for breaking them, a
strict curfew, chaotic sleeping conditions in crowded, bug-
infested barracks, bad food and too little of it, and armed
guards to enforce all of that.

Eva was assigned to jobs at the camp farm and garden. Her
daily life was sometimes dull and exhausting, sometimes frantic with fear. She made friends and lost them to disease or to
the mysterious "transports to Poland." She smuggled vegetables to her loved ones, learned to scrounge, scavenge, and

bribe. She heard news and rumors of the war with each train-load of new prisoners. She wondered whether her sweetheart was alive or dead.

And she kept a diary. It has turned out to be one of the important documents of that terrible time, a witness to some of the small events that went to make up the huge event we keep trying to understand.

Eva Roubíčková didn't build her diary like a story, with a series of characters and plot developments leading to a climax. Instead, she tried to keep track of the days as they went threat-eningly by. In her diary she confesses love and resentment, curiosity and frustration. She tells of smuggling potatoes under her clothes, of rivalries and kindnesses among inmates. She tells about being interrogated and going to prison. She wonders, "Can you turn thoughts off?" And she stubbornly refuses to give up the last threads of hope.

We have many different kinds of history. One kind tells how people with political power caused sweeping changes in the world. Another kind tells how their victims lived from one day to the next, how they rose to the tormenting occasion or sank beneath its weight. How they found ways to keep their feet warm and get enough potatoes to eat.

Eva Roubíčková's diary is that kind of history.

VIRGINIA EUWER WOLFF

AUTHOR'S NOTE

I WAS BORN ON JULY 16, 1921, into a German-speaking Jewish family in northern Bohemia, then part of the Sudetenland, in what is now the Czech Republic. My father was a professor of Latin and Greek at the gymnasium, the classical secondary school, in the town of Žatec (or Saaz, as it was called in German); my mother was a housewife and volunteer organist at the local synagogue. I attended the school where my father taught. We lived in a large house with my mother's mother and brother. My grandmother spent a lot of time with me and participated actively in my upbringing since my mother was only twenty-one when I was born. I was somewhat spoiled, being both an only child and an only grandchild, and I lived a charmed existence, playing tennis and swimming in summer and skiing in winter with my many Jewish and non-Jewish friends. But my carefree life gradually came to an end with Hitler's rise to power. As Nazi propaganda increased, I watched my non-Jewish friends grow ever more distant and estranged.

During the summer of 1938 I went to visit relatives in Plzeň (Pilsen), where I met many new people at a Jewish tennis club. Among them was Richard Roubíček, my future husband. I was seventeen, and since he was eleven years older and had finished his law degree, I thought of him only as a friend. Months later his sister told me that when he went back to Prague to visit his family, he announced he had met the girl he wished to marry. He had not told me.

Meanwhile, I had returned to Žatec, but with the beginning of the school year life became unbearable. Former friends—classmates and teachers alike—started treating all Jews as inferior. People stopped talking to us. We were forced to sit in the back of the classroom. Hitler made weekly speeches that were broadcast in the streets, and following each speech, men would march up and down, yelling anti-Semitic slogans and throwing rocks at the windows of Jewish houses and busi-nesses. Setting foot outside became a life-threatening experi-ence. I cried every morning at the thought of facing another day at school and every evening because of the awful things I had been through. My parents insisted that I continue my education, however, and my father continued teaching even though he was the only Jewish teacher at the school and was treated very badly by his colleagues and students.

In the middle of September my mother and grandmother went to Prague to rent a room in case things took a turn for the worse. The day after they returned, I came home from school in tears as usual, and they told me to pack a few things in my book bag: we were going to Prague for a few days. I was thrilled to have what I thought would be a brief vacation. I never returned. I left with my mother and grandmother; my father and uncle joined us a few days later. As a result of the Munich Agreement in September 1938, what was to be a brief break turned into a permanent situation.

Eva Glauber and her family will be mentioned frequently in the diary. I met Eva at the end of 1940 after we moved from our family home in Žatec to a one-room apartment in Prague. I didn't know anybody yet, and when I met Eva we immediately became close friends. Our friendship meant a great deal to me. Eva was intelligent, sensitive, and a very beautiful girl. She was also kind, tactful, and very talented artistically. She was the soul and center of a group of young people whom I frequently write about in the diary. This group met on a regular basis and we shared the traumas of that terrible time. Our friendship was my source of strength in Prague and later in Theresienstadt. Even now, years later, I firmly believe that Eva and the majority of the members in our group were not average people. Besides Eva and me, the group included both Grünberger brothers, Danny and Benny, Peter, and Zwi.

Since we were not allowed to wash our clothes or cook in the room we had rented, we were forced to look for other quarters and eventually found a place with a kitchen and bath. Friends took up collections for us, scraping together such basics as dishes and winter clothes. While in Prague, I happened to meet my friend Richard in the street. It turned out he had been searching for me. We were happy to find each other again and tried to lead a normal existence: I began attending school; Richard worked for his father's law firm.

But by this time all Jews were trying to emigrate. Richard's marriage proposal was a reflection of our times. Instead of saying, "Will you marry me?" he said, "Will you emigrate with me?" Because of my age I responded, "I'll have to ask my parents," whereupon Richard made a formal visit to them. My parents of course agreed to the marriage. Richard also introduced me to his family. I soon became close to them, and they were most kind and helpful to both me and my parents.

For a long time our attempts to obtain visas to a safe country were in vain. Finally, however, a week after Czechoslovakia was occupied by Nazi troops (March 15, 1939), Richard managed to secure permission to go to England. His intention was to arrange for all of us to follow. Both families saw him off at the station. My grandmother was inconsolable: she was afraid she would never see him again. That night, worried that her age would make her a burden to us, she committed suicide.

Richard succeeded in finding employment for me in England. I was to work as a nanny for an English family. Because I was not yet eighteen, however, the British refused to give me a work permit and I was unable to leave. Richard also arranged for his niece and nephew to live with an English family. They were due to leave on September 1, 1939, the day World War II broke out. They never left and perished with their mother in Auschwitz.

The years between the outbreak of the war and our departure for Theresienstadt saw increased restrictions for Jews. As of January 1939 I was forbidden to attend school and began learning to cook and make hats. All contact with foreign countries was outlawed, and with the exception of a few messages via Switzerland or America, I lost contact with Richard. Jews were no longer allowed to own businesses, earn money, or go to public places such as theaters or parks. They had to sew a yellow Star of David on their clothes and wear it at all times.

In October 1941 the first Jews left Prague in transports for Poland. All Jews had to register, and the atmosphere was one of fear and panic. The Jewish community organized the transports following German orders. Whenever somebody got the summons to go to the Messepalast for a transport, the Jewish community, friends, and family would go to that person's house and hide or distribute their valuables for them, and bring food, necessities, and sleeping bags. Rumors—both pessimistic and optimistic—ran rampant; nobody knew what to believe. Early in the fall of 1941 several thousand young men were sent to Theresienstadt, supposedly to build a Jewish ghetto. A few days later transports of a thousand people each began to depart for the new Theresienstadt ghetto. My mother and I left Prague in a transport on December 17.

MAP OF THE LOCATION OF THERESIENSTADT, 1939–1945, AND THE DEATH CAMPS OF POLAND

■ Transport Camp
▲ Death Camp

WE'RE ALIVE AND LIFE GOES ON

1941

DECEMBER 10, WEDNESDAY: I stayed home in the morning, went shopping in the afternoon, and came back. A half hour later Aunt Else phoned. We're in the next transport. I was quite calm about it and went immediately to the Jewish Community Center with Mommy to see if there is anything that can be done for us because of Daddy. Everyone at the community center was terribly worried; nobody knew anything, nobody had any advice. Mommy was upset. The Glasers and the Kohns came to see us; they're awfully upset too. At 11 P.M. a man from the community center came and laid out the situation in black and white for us. Just Mommy and I will be going. I couldn't sleep all night.

DECEMBER 11, THURSDAY: We started working again at four in the morning. We sewed sleeping bags. We visited Mama [Richard's mother] in the morning and then ran lots of errands. We worked at home in the afternoon. Lots of people came to visit us. Karl Reiner is trying to help us, but it's unclear whether he'll succeed.

DECEMBER 12, FRIDAY: I spent the entire morning at the community center. I got a number: 69. The mood wasn't quite as horrible and desperate as I'd expected. We're all in the same boat. Gi wants to sign up voluntarily, but first our appeal needs to be resolved. I was X-rayed at the clinic. If they found something, that would be another possibility. But you never know if you should play with destiny. The next transports are probably going to Poland after the New Year, but Theresienstadt is certainly much better. I spent the entire afternoon running from one clinic to the next. There was an incredible uproar everywhere, long lines everywhere, and we have so much to do at home! We're known everywhere as a special case because of Daddy. We're the only ones in this transport, so it's completely up to the Gestapo if they'll let us stay here with Daddy. We're touched by all our friends' kindness: Mama, the Glasers, and Frau Kohn, who has so much to do herself. We've been working day and night. Lots of times we thought we'd finished but then saw that the real work was still ahead of us. We got rid of everything in the apartment, stored things with Aryans, and sorted the food. That was most of the work. And throughout it all, the awful uncertainty of whether we're going or not. But we had to expect the answer would be yes. Poor Gi was the most upset of us all.

DECEMBER 13, SATURDAY: We started working again at 4 A.M. Peter and Danny came at 7 A.M. with the scale. We weighed all our things. We've got more than 100 pounds. The community center notified us in the morning that our appeal had been denied and that we had to go. Gi immediately volunteered to go as well. All our luggage was picked up in the morning. We cleaned the pantry in the afternoon. That was the hardest part. We got rid of much more in the evening and traded all the carpets and furniture. I felt paralyzed the entire day. Thank God there was no time to think about anything. It's as if somebody gave me a shot and I know it should hurt, but I can't feel a thing. Mama's with us all the time. Received photos from Richard. They're from Uncle Richard in America.

DECEMBER 14, SUNDAY: Took another bath in the morning and washed my hair. We had an awful lot of visitors and there's still so much more work, and on top of that I'm worried about Mommy. She's terribly upset and cries all the time, mostly because of Daddy. I wrote him a long letter, but it won't go out until we've left for the Messepalast. It's terrible for him, like getting hit by lightning. For God's sake, he shouldn't volunteer to go with us. It would be a catastrophe. Otto Mändl came to see us. Frau Glauber has sent us food every day. Mama came today and cooked for us. Though we had plenty of everything, we couldn't eat and had to force every bite down. We drove to the Messepalast at noon. Gi went to the community center. He doesn't have a number yet and doesn't know if he'll be included. Mama, Eva, Danny, and lots of others went along to keep us company. Good-bye, Prague. Just don't think! We had to register by 1 P.M. We quickly said good-bye to everybody. The gates closed behind us, and from now on we're prisoners; we're no longer free human beings.

The Messepalast is a huge wooden hall that's been divided into many sections. The first impression is terrible. I couldn't show how I really felt because of Mommy and tried to seem cheerful. The entire floor is covered with mattresses, with only a few narrow paths between them. We're on the mattresses day and night. Some of the people seem in a good mood, but others are horribly upset, unhappy, devastated. We belong to the first group. We went exploring right away. I saw a lot of people I knew: Egon Forscher, whom I'd once met at Benny's; a good friend of Zwi's named Pacovsky, who I went to school with in Saaz; and a nephew of the Taussigs. At four o'clock they brought in a man who looked deathly ill, with a wife in tears and a screaming child. They put them right next to us. On closer inspection we saw it was Paul Mändl. After a while we found out it was only an act they hoped would eventually get them sent home.

There's a girl (Fanny) my age on the other side of me. She seems very nice. I made friends with her immediately. She got married six weeks ago and voluntarily signed up to be with her husband. There are large pipes with faucets for washing at the side and to the front of the hall. On the other side is an open kitchen. There's a shed with a sink that the women use for washing clothes. The "nicest" part is the WC—a long wooden shed with buckets that need to be taken out daily. Everyone's disgusted and terribly unhappy about it. I don't really mind that much.

My new friend is with me all the time. I'm glad to have her. She's athletic and cheerful, and all of this is easier to take when you're with somebody. Egon visited us in the evening and stayed all night. I didn't sleep, and we stayed up talking all night.

DECEMBER 15, MONDAY: We had to turn in our house keys. Not us, of course, but Daddy, because he stayed home. Just keys to closets—to all those completely empty closets. We were ordered to turn in all our money, silver, etc. Fiedler, the man in charge of things here, came around several times to check on us. He's a twenty-three-year-old hoodlum who yells at everybody. His sidekick is Mandler, who's even worse. G. arrived in the evening. We were terribly happy.

I've been given a yellow armband. I've been given a kettle to heat water so people can wash themselves and wash dishes. It's a great job. I don't have to stand in line for food and sometimes even get two helpings. There's plenty of good food. In the morning there's black coffee and a stale roll, at noon soup and meat with a side dish, in the afternoon lime blossom tea, and in the evening soup or goulash. But it's best not to watch how they cook it.

DECEMBER 16, TUESDAY: I'm with Egon a lot and with a few other young people, but always with Fanny. I've written home twice now, once illegally to Eva, once legally to Mama. There was a terrible commotion this evening. Fiedler started slapping people around because somebody was smoking. All smoking items, money to the last cent, liquor, and other valuables had to be turned in. There was lots of screaming to get everybody scared and upset. But it was mostly Jews doing it. We were told they also spot-check people's luggage, and much slapping and beating goes along with that too. It was pouring rain just as we started to load the luggage. We kept very few things and even sent our sleeping bags ahead without sleeping in them on the last night.

DECEMBER 17, WEDNESDAY: We got up at six in the morning. Sleeping is awful. People walk around all night. Somebody's always coughing. Mommy slept horribly. I've fared better the last two nights. All the men had their heads shaved, but not the women. Everything was ready for departure by eight. At nine they led us to the station, heavily guarded by German soldiers carrying loaded guns. They put us into a sealed train, and at eleven we left for Theresienstadt. We're hideously squeezed together with all the luggage. It's all so strange; you simply can't understand it. Thank God, because if you could, you'd go crazy.

We arrived in Theresienstadt at two in the afternoon. We were welcomed by the emergency service. The boys looked pretty bad—not enough food, unshaven faces, shaved heads—but their mood wasn't all that bad. We had to go on foot from Bohušovice to Theresienstadt. Even though we didn't have much luggage, it was a terribly difficult walk. We were taken to the barracks and welcomed by lots of Jews, Rudy Lekner among them. He's changed, decidedly for the better. Fanny's husband and some of his friends took us to our room. It's a small room with running water and a nice heater. There are wood shavings on the floor. It's the Hohenelber barracks. It's a hospital, and we'll probably only stay here temporarily. The men are staying in the same barracks but in different rooms. There are eight of us. They all seem like very nice people.

DECEMBER 18, THURSDAY: We get black coffee in the morning, soup at noon, and soup in the evening. We're slowly settling in. The boys from the Sudeten barracks carried our luggage in. The poor fellows had so much to lug.

DECEMBER 19, FRIDAY: I talked to Benny in the morning. I was so happy. He carried suitcases too, but then sat with us all afternoon. Zwi came in the afternoon, and I spent the afternoon with both of them. Mommy had a bridge party.

DECEMBER 20, SATURDAY: A boy came early this morning with greetings from Zwi and a box of matches, which are an absolute necessity here, even though nobody's allowed to have them. Zwi has a permanent pass and can even go shopping. I was really glad. We did some morning gymnastics in the yard under German surveillance. Cigarettes are in great demand here. They're even more valuable than bread. Everybody's crazy about them, and there are people smoking everywhere, even though it's strictly forbidden. Zwi and Benny came to visit me in the afternoon. Our room looks really nice.

We can heat it, and we don't fight like the others. The boys and girls behave terribly here. We suddenly got an order at ten. The women have to move out of the Hohenelber barracks by tomorrow morning. A man was found together with his wife and was arrested immediately, so now all of us have to move. We packed at night and were up again by 5 A.M.

DECEMBER 21, SUNDAY: It's Fanny's birthday. We spent the morning sitting on our suitcases until they took us to our new barracks. We had to stand outside a long while. There was lots of commotion. Our room wanted to stay together. Do what you like, but don't make us room with old people! They let us inside, and we all ran to grab a room. There was no order whatsoever. Whoever knew somebody in the barracks got a nice room. In the end, we alone were without a room. We kept going into rooms with people already in them, and they'd throw us out. Finally we were given a huge freezing room. The situation was hopeless. Everybody was crying. Zwi managed to grab my two bags of food and get them back to me. We sat on our luggage, fought for space. We were freezing, hungry, and about to go crazy. We were completely shut off from the world, no help anywhere, no way out.

This was the worst day yet since the evacuation. They were looking for a room leader, and I was selected. At least I had something to do right away. I had to take down everybody's name, etc., and so the worst was over. The barracks were ancient. In the morning they told us they were the most modern barracks, with central heating, hot water, and everything else, but nobody's ever seen those things. We gradually thawed out as the room heated up. Then some food came from the Hohenelber barracks. Each of us got a mattress. It was not very comfortable to sleep on.

DECEMBER 22, MONDAY: Constant running around with our luggage. We have a fairly decent bathroom with cold water. They're setting up an office.

DECEMBER 23, TUESDAY: I've got lots of running around to do as room elder, that is, as room youngest. I'm still with Fanny all the time. We do everything together. I'm so lucky to have her. Of couse Mommy's always with us too. Every day we have to check in with the office. They tell us what we can and cannot do. All the room elders are there, and it's quite interesting. I spoke to Mio. It made me so happy. He was here with some suitcases. He looked fabulous, but I almost didn't recognize him. He's big and strong and seems to be doing well. Somebody brought me a letter from Gi. He does pedicures and is very busy. Fanny's husband is here every day. He comes with the cleaning crew. They're just about the only men we talk to. In a few days we'll be able to cook here. Fanny, Paula, and I are always together. We've volunteered to peel potatoes. It's not the most pleasant job, but it may be an opportunity to get into the kitchen, which of course would be ideal.

DECEMBER 24, WEDNESDAY: Besides coffee, soup, and a potato for lunch, and soup or coffee for dinner, Mommy and I get a slice of bread to share every other day. We've given away most of the bread we brought from Prague. The poor fellows were so hungry. I don't know how we'll manage with the rations. For now we still have some crackers and pumpernickel bread, but what will happen when they're gone? Well, we'll manage somehow. We're supposed to get up every day at six in the morning, but of course we don't. They've set up a home for boys and they'll make another one for girls, but at the moment there's a scarlet fever epidemic. They'll probably use our room for it, and we'll have to move again. Horrible. Today's order is to turn in all canned goods, tea, medicines, and perfumes in addition to the things we've already turned in. And, of course, cigarettes, matches, money, jewels, etc. The worst thing is the request to give up canned goods. Of course we're not going to turn them in, and we won't eat them the way the others do. It's Christmas Eve.

DECEMBER 25, THURSDAY: The housing situation is making us desperate. All the rooms are overcrowded. They'll probably put each of us in different rooms. We can't unpack anything and never have a moment's peace. By January 1 everything is supposed to be turned in, and now we don't even have a place to hide stuff. We're constantly looking for a new room. Mommy finally found a room with two other ladies. It has a stone floor and no heat. We wouldn't have minded that, but they didn't let us keep it anyway. Fanny, Paula, and I peel potatoes every day, and it's not so bad. I have a lot of writing and paperwork to do as room elder during my free time. We always need something.

DECEMBER 26, FRIDAY: With the exception of the toilet cleaners, we don't get to talk to any men. Benny came with the crew today. I was overjoyed! A ghetto guard and a fireman also came. I coincidentally became friends with a fellow who has a permanent pass, and he immediately handed me a sack of clothes to wash for him. I offered to do laundry for all the boys. It's not such a hard job, and the poor boys really have no idea how to go about it.

DECEMBER 27, SATURDAY: We finally have a room, but it doesn't have heat yet. A couple of older ladies have moved, but we still sleep in the old room. I've lost my watch. There's very little food, but it's bearable. We still have some left from home.

I don't wear dresses at all, only slacks. Unfortunately I only brought a few pairs, and no decent ones. A man offered to send letters for us. I wrote to Mama. Although that means the death penalty, everybody writes anyway. Actually I imagined that being in a ghetto would be much worse, sort of like death, in that you can't really conceive what it's like. When we first saw the people who've been here for a while, they seemed to come from another world. But we live here too, and we're not in too terrible a mood. We even laugh quite often, which I wouldn't have considered possible in Prague. In short, life goes on. You just can't allow yourself to think about anything. We're busy all day, and then at night we lie on the mattresses and sleep. Just don't think. Anything but that! We even talk to boys.

DECEMBER 28, SUNDAY: We've finally settled into the room we fought so hard for. It's a passageway to where the old ladies are. We immediately made partitions with our blankets. There are six of us. We've barely enough space. We're happy, though, because at least we can get organized. Things are slowly working themselves out. I do laundry for a whole bunch of boys. You can even begin to see a certain organization in it all, even though we're lacking everything. The most important things just aren't available—brooms and dustpans, for example, and much more.

DECEMBER 29, MONDAY: The three of us busily peel potatoes and sort potatoes in the basement besides. It's a terrible job—cold, dark, and dirty. Mommy peels potatoes too, but not when we're there. We've made a table from our suitcases. We tolerate each other fairly well. Compared with the other rooms, it's ideal. Women are fighting terribly everywhere. We're somewhat calmer here than we were in Prague, where we were only half alive from the terrible fear. That's all behind us now. What else can happen to us?

DECEMBER 30, TUESDAY: We're guarded by police, who for the most part are quite decent. Lots of men come from the Hohenelber barracks every day. Sometimes they're not allowed to talk to the women at all; then they're allowed to again. The women housed in the Dresden barracks are never allowed to talk to men. Everything's much stricter there. Any man caught talking to a woman is given twenty-five lashes with a whip. The food here is also slightly better than elsewhere. Children often get different and better food than we do.

DECEMBER 31, WEDNESDAY: I already know lots of people here. We're on a first-name basis, and it's quite friendly. Until now people were allowed to receive packages. Lots of people got them. We didn't. But starting today, all packages and letters are prohibited, because there was always some stupid person who wrote careless letters. One man was arrested for three months because of it. Fanny and I are known as the two hungriest souls of all the transports. New Year's Eve was celebrated in several rooms. We didn't celebrate—we weren't in the mood. Paula brought four men from the firefighters group to us at midnight even though we were already asleep. Supposedly to bring us luck. We could use it.

1942

JANUARY 1, THURSDAY: We've piled up everything we're supposed to turn in but haven't yet agreed on where to hide it. There was a concert in the office this afternoon. Somebody played the accordion, and somebody else sang. It was just like the old days. It was a strange feeling. Lots of people cried. We sang Czech and German songs. Fredy Hirsch gave a speech. He dared to say a lot of things, like that we're at our lowest point now, that soon things will be better, and that there was never a ruler who lasted forever. About halfway through we had to stop, and all the men had to leave. The police broke it up.

JANUARY 2, FRIDAY: I already know lots of people. Fanny and I manage, more or less honestly, to get things to eat. There isn't enough food, but most people still have rations from home. I have made lots of friends doing laundry for the boys. I get along really well with the electricians, the custodial crew, and lots of others. Zwi came to visit me. We keep in touch by writing frequently.

JANUARY 3, SATURDAY: Frau Kraus is the only one in our room who fights all the time. She argues about the heat every day. Mommy has to bring her coffee every morning. Where does she get her nerve?

■   ■   ■

JANUARY 4, SUNDAY: Everybody's upset. A transport is leaving from here for Poland. Will we be in it? It's horrible. We thought we'd be secure here, but from now on it'll be exactly the way it was in Prague. They called out names in the afternoon, and the following day the people had to be ready. Frau Kauders voluntarily signed up to be with her husband. Nobody else from our barracks is going. We spent half the night getting her packed.

JANUARY 5, MONDAY: Fanny and I have kitchen duty. We take turns standing by the kitchen door and aren't allowed to let anybody in. We're happy since we get food and can even take some home. It's strictly forbidden, but of course we don't care. The morning transport was taken to the Hamburg barracks. The people all looked horrible—sick and old, with torn suitcases and no food.

JANUARY 6, TUESDAY: Kitchen duty's great. Even though we have to be there all the time, morning till night, fight with people who want to come in, and get in trouble with the kitchen crew if we do let someone in, it's worth it. The general mood is very bad. Many people go to the Hamburg barracks to peel potatoes to have someone to talk to.

JANUARY 7, WEDNESDAY: I have an admirer, an electrician. Zwi and Benny are here every day and they always get something to eat.

JANUARY 8, THURSDAY: Nine people who were jailed for smuggling letters have been hanged. Jews had to perform the execution. There's much desperation everywhere.

■　　　■　　　■

JANUARY 9, FRIDAY: All the room elders were called to a meeting in the Magdeburg barracks. They made a beautiful speech about how the executions were only supposed to serve as a deterrent.

JANUARY 10, SATURDAY: Another transport is going to Poland. Nobody knows for sure where in Poland they're going. Some people say Riga, others say Josefstadt. Only two old ladies from our transport were included. One of them started screaming hysterically. It's a disaster.

JANUARY 12, MONDAY: Lots of commotion first thing in the morning. More women were summoned for the transport. Almost half of them were from our barracks. By chance we weren't included. Whoever you spoke to was in the transport. There was chaos everywhere. They had three hours to get packed. Mommy, Fanny, and I are the only ones left in the room.

JANUARY 13, TUESDAY: This morning they summoned an additional fifty women to the transport, because lots of the Protectorate children were pulled out again. I got a letter from Zwi. He wants to protect us from Poland by registering me to work in the farms, possibly even as his fiancée. It's only a formality, of course, but it's awfully decent of him.

JANUARY 14, WEDNESDAY: Thank God, nobody else has been summoned. Benny, Zwi, and many others come to visit me. There's an advantage to working in the kitchen—at least we always have something for the boys to eat.

JANUARY 15, THURSDAY: Nepotism rules everywhere here. There's no other way. Everybody's out for himself. There's a lively black market in cigarettes and food.

JANUARY 16, FRIDAY: We're expecting three new transports from Pilsen, and probably more will leave here for Poland. Nobody knows where the last two went.

JANUARY 17, SATURDAY: I now have a steady job with the gardeners. I'm already looking forward to the spring when we can work outdoors. Mommy plays bridge in the afternoon sometimes.

JANUARY 18, SUNDAY: The first transport from Pilsen arrived. I went to peel potatoes in the Hamburg barracks. Nobody we knew came.

JANUARY 19, MONDAY: They're doing inspections in the Sudeten barracks. We're really scared. We put everything into a suitcase with a false number on it. I had to repack everything. Working in the kitchen takes a lot of time, and in my free time I do laundry for a lot of people and have lots of visitors.

JANUARY 20, TUESDAY: I think we're going to have to move into the Hamburg barracks.

JANUARY 21, WEDNESDAY: The second Pilsen transport arrived. People were in terrible shape. They've been whipped for no reason. Zwi brought me two spoons we'd lost. It's horribly cold.

JANUARY 22, THURSDAY: We'll be moving on Sunday. Everybody's getting ready and arranging who they want to room with. We're afraid we won't be able to work in the kitchen anymore.

JANUARY 23, FRIDAY: The third Pilsen transport is coming on Monday. We're packing for the Hamburg barracks.

JANUARY 24, SATURDAY: Last time in the kitchen. I ate a lot. Who knows what the food situation will be like in the Hamburg barracks.

JANUARY 25, SUNDAY: We moved our luggage into the Hamburg barracks in the morning. Mommy saved a space for us there. We went back and forth with the luggage three times. We're in a large room with twenty-two people. Marcel reserved spaces for us. The people seem quite nice.

JANUARY 26, MONDAY: The third transport from Pilsen arrived. There are almost only old and sick people. Aunt Gretl and Uncle Rudi, Nelly, and Herr Popper were in it. It's horribly cold. They all arrived in terrible shape. Benny and I went from room to room and told everybody not to turn anything in.

JANUARY 27, TUESDAY: Fanny and I are on meal duty. We go from room to room, calling people to lunch and dinner, and get larger portions. It's almost better than kitchen duty since we do a few hours' work and then are free. Mommy's peeling potatoes again and has taken charge of the old-age home.

JANUARY 28, WEDNESDAY: Life in the barracks is not as easy as it was before. Everything is so terribly spread out. Nepotism rules, and if you don't take care of everything yourself, you won't get anything at all. There are always meetings being called, everything is taken so seriously, and at the same time meal duty's a joke.

JANUARY 29, THURSDAY: Marcel comes here almost every day, and so do Benny and Zwi. One of the boys brought a harmonica and played it, but a ghetto guard came and told him, "You have to stop this instant. Somebody reported it."

JANUARY 30, FRIDAY: Another transport arrived from Prague today. I went from room to room again. The Sgalitzers came and brought a package from Mama.

JANUARY 31, SATURDAY: All the men from sanitation and meal duty have to leave the barracks. It's just like in the Dresden barracks now, where only some men are allowed into the barracks. A few small rooms even have stoves. Our room is horrible. Everybody from the office [Jewish Council of Elders] was fired. Fanny has really disappointed me. She's very calculating and only associates with people she can profit from. She's had lots of advantages being with us. Mommy shared everything with her and brought her coffee every morning. Fanny also got a lot from her husband and never shared even the slightest bit with us. She would hide everything and make it a secret so she wouldn't have to share.

FEBRUARY 1, SUNDAY: A transport arrived from Brünn—almost all young people who were in good shape. I spent a lot of time with Aunt Gretl. She brought lots of food with her and refuses to eat the food here. She can't even imagine what it's like to be hungry. I'm on meal duty with Emmi at lunch. She's very nice. Doing laundry here is a disaster. We're not allowed to hang it anywhere, and I still get lots of it from the boys I'd been doing it for in the Bodenbacher barracks. I'm going to have to stop now.

FEBRUARY 3, TUESDAY: Once a week we get eleven pounds of jam for dessert. Mommy's busy rationing, so we manage quite well with food. Besides that, Mommy's usually able to take a couple of potatoes. She also gets food for the old ladies morning, noon, and night, and they give her some.

■   ■   ■

FEBRUARY 4, WEDNESDAY: They're opening a laundry soon, and they'll be looking for people to work there. We're allowed to write home now but not to get packages. Of course we have to be really careful about what we write. Fanny's very selfish. Most of the girls here are loose, so they get what they want from the boys. I can't do that, and I'll never get anything. Zwi and Benny come to visit me often. They aren't getting along as well as they used to.

FEBRUARY 5, THURSDAY: Three-quarters of the women here don't have periods. The last time for me was on the way to Theresienstadt.

FEBRUARY 6, FRIDAY: The women in our room are very pleasant, especially Frau Koralek. She's such a decent person and has everything you could imagine.

FEBRUARY 7, SATURDAY: Marcel visits me every day. He's extremely kind, but so clumsy. Aunt Gretl's often with us. She's slowly beginning to understand the situation here and eats everything they give her now.

FEBRUARY 8, SUNDAY: Another transport arrived from Prague. We know some of the people, but they've brought us nothing. Why doesn't anyone send us anything? Don't they know we're going hungry here?

FEBRUARY 11, WEDNESDAY: I wonder whether the letters have arrived in Prague. God knows how long it takes them to get there. The great optimism of the first few weeks has noticeably cooled off. Nobody's counting anymore on getting home by spring. It'll be interesting to remember all of this one day. I go to Budíček and line up for coal at six every morning, line up for meals, and it's a fight for every single inch of space. Each person's allotted only two feet. We fight for mattresses. It's very cold every night.

FEBRUARY 12, THURSDAY: The biggest farce is the custodial crew, which is a bunch of young, pretty girls who just want to stand around all day amusing themselves. Their leader is A., who dances around the barracks as if she were a circus director.

FEBRUARY 13, FRIDAY: The supply situation is also interesting. If you want to eat, you have to get the ghetto guard involved. The electric cookers are a big problem. They short-circuit all the time, and they'll probably be forbidden. That would be terrible, because there's nowhere for us to warm our food.

FEBRUARY 19, THURSDAY: A Prague transport arrived. Aunt Flora was in it. Mommy's still bedridden, though she's getting better. Aunt Flora's in a good mood and hasn't changed.

FEBRUARY 20, FRIDAY: Aunt Gretl's just like us now, hungry all the time, and so is Aunt Flora. We got some cheese and a bit of fat from her. I've received orders to start work tomorrow as a gardener. I'm very happy about it, but it'll certainly be harder to get food once I stop doing meal duty.

FEBRUARY 21, SATURDAY: It's not so easy to get out of meal duty. I'll have to write an appeal. This afternoon I went to the greenhouse in the Hohenelber barracks for the first time with the group. It felt strange to be walking on the street again. There are six of us, and we went unaccompanied. Steffi is the group leader. We picked lettuce and radishes in the greenhouse.

FEBRUARY 26, THURSDAY: Another ten people were executed, some for smuggling letters, others for fighting back when Seidl beat them. The mood is dreadful everywhere again.

FEBRUARY 27, FRIDAY: It's a huge drawback that I'm not doing meal duty anymore. I only get small portions now. We ration here and there, but not a lot. Sometimes Zwi brings me food.

FEBRUARY 28, SATURDAY: Bathed for the first time this afternoon. It was a glorious feeling to lie in a tub. Spent time with the gardeners afterward.

MARCH 5, THURSDAY: A crew is being assembled to go to Germany. The German director who inspects the garden twice a day is quite nice and very satisfied with us.

MARCH 6, FRIDAY: The officers' garden is outside of Theresienstadt. It has a large greenhouse and a garden that's been completely renovated. Zwi has changed a lot in the last few days. He hardly speaks to me.

MARCH 7, SATURDAY: The next Poland transport has been set up. It has mostly people from the Kladno transport.

MARCH 8, SUNDAY: A supplement to the Poland transport was added this morning. Uncle Viktor's in it, and Aunt Flora immediately volunteered. She had to get ready within an hour and by midmorning was on the train. Mommy and Aunt Gretl helped her.

MARCH 11, WEDNESDAY: Spent time with my Komotauer relatives. They're completely helpless. They've moved into a small room. One of the daughters is sick. As of June they plan to open the ghetto. All Aryans will have to move out of Theresienstadt.

MARCH 12, THURSDAY: Two hundred men have been assigned to work the mines at Kladno for the second time. Everybody envies them. They'll certainly be better off, have a freer life and more to eat. Still, we haven't heard any news from there at all.

MARCH 15, MONDAY:[1] The food situation is dreadful. Mommy gets a ration and I get a ration. Sometimes Mommy makes something out of the potatoes. Egon lives right next to the garden, with twenty-eight pigs. He's doing very well.

MARCH 17, WEDNESDAY: Worked in the greenhouse at municipal headquarters. It's a very beautiful greenhouse with flowers and leafy plants. An Aryan works as a gardener there. I'm helping out again at meals and get larger rations. Things simply aren't possible any other way.

MARCH 23, TUESDAY: The Brünn transport arrived. Egon's love is here now. She's going to tend the pigs too. Poor Gi's really hungry, and it's tormenting him. We often send him things but have so little ourselves.

MARCH 27, SATURDAY: The Poland transport has been summoned. Gi's in it. Mommy's frantic. This afternoon we

---

[1] Eva did not have a calendar and had no way to make sure her days and dates were right. March 15 was a Sunday. From time to time there are other similar slips. Since Eva cannot recall now which is correct—day or date—the entries have been left as she wrote them.

tried to get inside the Magdeburg barracks. We didn't make it. Gi visited us. He's completely calm. He's reconciled to leaving even though he's written a petition.

MARCH 28, SUNDAY: I visited Mommy and the coal crew in the Magdeburg this afternoon. Spent the afternoon with Gi. There are a bunch of young boys in Fredy Hirsch's room who act like big men here. Gi's in a good mood. He's certain he'll be going. He went to the commission that puts the transports together to see whether his petition went through but couldn't get any information.

MARCH 29, MONDAY: A thousand women are going to Pürglitz. Should I sign up with Mommy? Maybe it would be better there. The transport has been set up. Mommy's in it, but I'm not, because I'm a gardener. Gi visited us in the afternoon, and from here he'll go directly to the sluice [transport assembly area]. Maybe I'll never see him again. Mommy's frantic.

MARCH 30, TUESDAY: Spoke to Wilda in the garden about what I should do with Mommy. If she goes, I'll voluntarily sign up no matter what. We absolutely have to stay together. Everybody says it would be insane for me to leave the garden. Wilda wants to pull all three mothers out of the transport. If he succeeds, she'll be protected from all further transports. Mommy doesn't quite know what to do. She'd really like to go to Pürglitz, yet wants me to stay in the garden. No news at all from Gi. Benny visits us every day. He's truly a good friend, and I can discuss everything with him.

MARCH 31, WEDNESDAY: Gi's out! He wrote us a letter right away, but we didn't receive it. We're overjoyed.

■   ■   ■

APRIL 1, THURSDAY: We still don't know if Mommy's out of the transport or not. We're busy preparing for Pürglitz. Fanny's unhappy because her husband is staying here. Our leader, Steffi, has also volunteered for Pürglitz.

APRIL 2, FRIDAY: Gi's with us. We're very happy. I'm working in a new garden that Porges has taken over.

APRIL 3, SATURDAY: Mommy's out of Pürglitz. I'm so glad. She has mixed feelings. She'd have liked to go because everybody says it's better there. The Brünn transport arrives this afternoon. It was difficult for me to get into the Cavalier barracks this afternoon.

APRIL 4, SUNDAY: Benny visited us this afternoon. We talked about normal times.

APRIL 5, MONDAY: Steffi doesn't go to the garden anymore. I'm leading the group now and using her pass until I get a new one. We planted lettuce the entire day. It's very strenuous work.

APRIL 6, TUESDAY: We received cards from Prague. I planted lettuce and am dead tired. The final Brünn transport has left. There are now officially no more Jews in Brünn (*judenrein*).

APRIL 7, WEDNESDAY: The Poland transport's been summoned. It has mostly people from the new Brünn transport. There aren't enough, so they'll have to take some from the old transports. The Pürglitz transport leaves on the tenth. An eight-year-old German rascal ran through everybody's rooms this evening, just as we were getting undressed. I don't know how they do it, but most of the people here manage to get at least something. It's terribly sad that the only way to get anything is through lying, stealing, and cheating. Will it ever be possible for us to fit back into normal life? Will we ever be normal, decent people again? Won't we all be criminals by the time we get out of here?

APRIL 9, SUNDAY: Used the pass this afternoon for the first time to enter the Dresden barracks. I visited Frau Adler and Käthe. They were both overjoyed. The Dresden is much worse than the Hamburg, or at least it seemed so to me.

APRIL 10, MONDAY: 3 A.M. departure for Pürglitz. They drove off in high spirits, and it made you really feel like going with them. I work very hard in the garden but see that it's being acknowledged. Zwi's talking to me again. I don't know what I've done to deserve such an honor. Benny spends time with us almost every day. He eats lunch with us in the barracks, because our food is much better than in the Cavalier.

APRIL 11, TUESDAY: I'm really glad that Fanny's gone. We hadn't gotten along lately and only spoke to each other out of necessity. We did some gymnastics in the evening. It was a stupid thing to do, especially since we're so tired when we come home from work.

APRIL 12, THURSDAY: Fanny's husband has volunteered to go to Poland. Something unusual must have happened. He probably stole something.

APRIL 13, FRIDAY: Got a pass in my name plus five more for two weeks.

■   ■   ■

APRIL 14, SATURDAY: We have lots of evidence that Fanny and her husband have stolen things, including my watch, which I thought I'd lost. Fanny had stolen some things from us in the Messepalast. We should file a report immediately so they'll search his luggage before he leaves for Poland.

APRIL 15, SUNDAY: The Poland transport left. Friedl has escaped from us. I visited Käthe in the afternoon at the Dresden barracks. She's living with a young girl who runs the nursery and is doing quite well. Gi and Benny visited us in the evening. We went for a walk in Theresienstadt with Mommy, Frau Gross, and Lotte. All of us felt elated.

APRIL 17, TUESDAY: The Poland transport left. Lots of people from our room were in it. Many of them were friends.

APRIL 18, WEDNESDAY: I worked in the garden and meal duty. At least that way you can sort of get enough to eat. Mommy looks awfully bad.

APRIL 19, THURSDAY: There's such an awful lot of corruption here, and only bad people prosper. Only if you steal, if you're brutal, or if you're a flirt can you get somewhere. If you can't, you might just as well starve. I simply can't use people or be calculating, and I'll never learn how. I work hard and let myself be used.

APRIL 20, FRIDAY: Tilling the soil is hard work. I'm dead tired.

APRIL 22, SUNDAY: I stayed in bed. I had my period for the first time in five months. Benny visited me. The Poland transport has left.

APRIL 23, MONDAY: I'm still in bed. I feel terrible. Gi visited us.

APRIL 24, TUESDAY: I'm getting a reputation for being a hard worker. A transport was set up last night and gone by early morning. Again many from our room.

APRIL 25, WEDNESDAY: This month there will be three more transports. Gi's with us every day. He may have to go away too. We were given a solid promise from both the director and Seidl that we won't be sent away. A bunch of us were pulled out.

APRIL 26, THURSDAY: The mood is dreadful everywhere. Everybody's packing and getting ready, because each of us must expect to go. A transport arrived but passed us by. It brought an awful lot of baggage.

APRIL 27, FRIDAY: Lots of older transports were summoned in the night and were gone by early morning. Half our room was in them.

APRIL 28, SATURDAY: Transports were summoned all night again. I didn't sleep all night. I waited to find out what's happening with Gi. A hideous night. Everybody had to report by 6 A.M. At seven I got a card from Gi. He had to go. Mommy's nerves are completely shot. She cries all the time. At least at work I'm able to think about other things.

APRIL 30, MONDAY: Another transport left for Poland early in the morning. Most of the people are from the Prague transports that just arrived.

■   ■   ■

MAY 4, FRIDAY: There's a terrible water shortage. We stand in long lines for every drop. Bathing is prohibited.

MAY 5, SATURDAY: We're getting an eighth of a loaf of bread per week now. It's not a lot, but better than nothing.

MAY 7, MONDAY: A Poland transport left. It was a combination of both Prague transports. Mommy's taken charge of the potato peelers. It's very hard work, but we expect much good to come from it. It's easier for her to take potatoes, and she'll have a better connection to the kitchen. We hope so, at least. She still takes food to the old women at lunch and dinner. She has an awful lot of work. Will it be worth it?

MAY 8, TUESDAY: Eva Müller's supposed to be dismissed from the garden. But she's very lazy. There are three well-connected girls with the gardeners. They aren't there the whole day but are credited for working ten hours, get as many radishes as they want, and probably get other things as well. One of them often goes to the German administrator's to cook and clean.

MAY 9, WEDNESDAY: We went to Bohušovice. Tonda Bischitzki made a huge stink because we didn't have our tools with us. We were sent home and put under house arrest for the entire day. We took it all rather lightly.

MAY 10, THURSDAY: It's scandalous what goes on in the kitchen. Friends of cooks get triple or even quadruple portions, and whoever makes eyes at the cook does too. Mommy doesn't get anything from the kitchen anymore and is disappointed. Now we're completely dependent on leftovers from the old ladies. That way Mommy has something to eat and I can have her portion.

MAY 11, FRIDAY: Twelve boys including Benny have moved to the citadel. It ought to be much better for them there. This evening Edelstein gave an interesting lecture. People are talking everywhere about plans for the ghetto when it's opened. Every day you can see cars loaded up with possessions of people moving away from here. I'm very curious. I hope it'll be better. It would be good if the whole garden group moved in together. Then maybe we could even get some more food.

MAY 12, SATURDAY: The food has improved a bit since the beginning. Sometimes we have dumplings. Once we even had dumplings and cakes. Mommy gets potatoes every day, but we have nowhere to cook them. We should always have something for supper; otherwise we eat too much bread.

MAY 16, WEDNESDAY: The food has improved a bit. I know two of the cooks, and when I take them chives, I sometimes get larger portions.

MAY 19, SATURDAY: The people living in our room are really disgusting. There's constant bickering.

MAY 22, TUESDAY: Only my group is allowed to work in the garden. Everybody else was fired for stealing lettuce. Now we're the permanent garden group. Huge commotion: the police have arrested several Jews. Transports with distinguished Jews are now arriving from Germany.

■   ■   ■

MAY 25, FRIDAY: I went to the bathing area to take a shower in the afternoon.

MAY 27, SUNDAY: I went with Edith this afternoon to visit the boys at the citadel. They have a good thing going for them. We were scared because girls aren't actually allowed in. At noon we were unexpectedly given notice to move our baggage within the hour because we're getting beds. This afternoon went to Porges's garden with Milena and two other girls. Erna Thieben's always nice company, and Karel Pollak played the harmonica. This evening we fought over beds. We're lying by the window in the middle level. There's no room for baggage. We fight over every centimeter. I took it with humor. What else can I do?

MAY 28, MONDAY: Magda, Kapp, and I are trying to get a room just for the gardeners and see Goldscheider every day about it. The beds are really abominable. Food's also a problem. Mommy can only get a little bit from the old ladies. I can get a larger portion if I know the cook.

MAY 29, TUESDAY: Goldscheider seems to have approved the room for us. We go there every day. We're harvesting lettuce in the garden. We get some every day. I usually trade it for bread, so now we have almost enough.

MAY 31, THURSDAY: I ate kohlrabi while harvesting it. Our *parta* [work crew] has made a resolution not to steal. We're quite a good *parta,* and we stick together. I'm the group leader. Even though all of us are often hungry, none of us steals anything, except for one girl who we're all angry with. We can finally move into the room tomorrow. The beds are terrible— you can't even move in them, let alone get to your things.

JUNE 1, FRIDAY: The people who are supposed to move out of the room are making trouble. They don't want to leave. Still, we were able to move in this afternoon.

JUNE 4, MONDAY: I went to pick cherries. I didn't even know there were any. It was a wonderful feeling to be perched on top of the tree. I took some for Mommy too.

JUNE 5, TUESDAY: Wilda is letting us pick cherries as a special reward. We're the only ones in all of Theresienstadt who have cherries. I picked eighty-eight pounds today.

JUNE 6, WEDNESDAY: Tonight Wilda told me and Eliska to come early and tend the geese.

JUNE 7, THURSDAY: There weren't any geese there yet, just goats and kids. They're supposedly from Lidice. The goats needed to be milked right away. A lot of people were there to milk them. I tried too, but it's not that easy.

JUNE 8, FRIDAY: Two hundred geese arrived. They were in terrible condition, like a Jewish transport. I'd like to stay here, but they won't let us because they need us in the garden.

JUNE 9, SATURDAY: A Poland transport was summoned. Everyone from Pürglitz is in it, but there are lots of gardeners too. It's a dreadful mess, and it's uncertain whether they'll get out.

JUNE 10, SUNDAY: Ely Bock was taken out of the transport and got married in the afternoon. They need more people for the transport. A hundred sheep arrived. Just the three of us,

Eliška, Milena, and I, did all the work, though Milena's mother and Frau Klinger helped.

JUNE 11, MONDAY: Vera Schulz and Trude Zolisch came to see us. Milking is working out quite well, and we don't need Tonda's help anymore. Eliška has let us down. She's acting like a streetwalker with Tonda and Wilda, and both Bischitzkis, whom I've always looked up to, are falling for it. The result is she doesn't have to lift a finger anymore.

JUNE 13, WEDNESDAY: Kraus the engineer has taken over as our supervisor. We're very glad somebody's got the responsibility.

JUNE 14, THURSDAY: I can cook potatoes in the kettle we use to steam peels for the geese. We have enough potatoes. Mommy takes a lot from the cellar.

JUNE 30, SUNDAY: I've gotten quite friendly with Vera. Milena, on the other hand, is always in a terrible mood and isn't very well liked. Eliška complains of a different ailment every day and always has an excuse not to work. I have lots of work. Kraus is quite good to have for a boss. One hundred twenty more sheep have arrived.

JULY 15, WEDNESDAY: Mommy was caught taking potatoes while peeling them and isn't allowed back anymore. She's unhappy because she doesn't know what kind of work she's going to get. She looks very bad. Maybe a different job will be better for her. Thank God I can always take something home, so it isn't such a pressing issue. As of August 1, the ghetto will be opened. There are big changes in Theresienstadt. All houses have been released to the Jews. Every week there are two Prague transports. They have almost only old people in them, then later members of the AK [*Aufbaukommando*], too. Grandma Gibian arrived, then a week later Grandmother Raubitschek. Grandma's in very bad shape. She didn't recognize me and spoke incoherently, and she didn't know where she was or what had happened to her. She was moved into a blockhouse. I wanted to get her luggage and came to the Hannover barracks just as it was being confiscated. I saved her little suitcase, an old aunt's suitcase, and both of Grandma Gibian's suitcases. I went to Jirka's room and gave them to a boy who works with us. The next day they said there would be an inspection, so we smuggled them past a very decent policeman and hid them in the goose shed outside of Theresienstadt. The constant fear! Frau Goldschmiedt came with a package from Mama. Grandma Gibian was moved to the infirmary. She's already recovered from the first shock. Grandmother Raubitschek died. Frau Erba arrived in good spirits, brave, and really happy to see me. She fed me all sorts of things and three days later was on her way to Poland. I didn't even have a chance to say good-bye. Everyone's allowed to leave the barracks now from 6 to 9 P.M. Men are allowed to visit their wives and vice versa. I spend a lot of time with Grandma Gibian. I got two puddings on the eve of my birthday and a bag with my name and transport number on it, and some pastries too.

JULY 16, THURSDAY: Every week two transports arrive from Prague. I'm expecting Mama and Daddy.

AUGUST 15, SATURDAY: I happened to be at the railway station by chance, but instead of Daddy, I found the Glaubers. I stayed with them and took their luggage. Benny saved their suitcase. He's incredibly ingenious. I haven't been very close with Benny lately—he has a girlfriend here. But we're renewing our friendship. Kraus's parents arrived. They could move to the sheep shed right away. It's a good place with a room and entryway. Sometimes I tend the geese or sheep, and sometimes I work at home. The geese get potatoes, and of course we get some too. We go to the garden every day for the leafy vegetables and take some home. I'm working steadily at the sheep stall and am my own boss. The others envy me because Kraus has taken me in, but I don't care. Kraus isn't the boss he used to be. He uses us, and nobody but me gets anything from him anymore. He's very selfish. He's got eggs, milk, and a lot of different things and doesn't allow the girls to have any of it. I go milking every day and take some to Mommy. It's insanely risky. If Kraus were to find out, I'd be fired from the farm immediately. But I have to do it. Mommy needs it, and now that she's been getting milk, she's been looking better, and that's more important than anything else.

We're slowly getting used to ghetto life. Mommy was doing emergency work for the transports every other night, but she's now working steadily as a nurse in the recovery room at our barracks. She's quite satisfied. I'm with the Glaubers every day. I convinced Tonda to let Eva work in the garden. She was approved within two weeks. She works in the field and likes it very much.

Daddy arrived on the August 13 transport. I was expecting him, but not really. The gardener group notified me earlier of it. Benny recognized him immediately from his photo. Everybody's been acting wonderfully toward him and me. I went to the sluice with him, and we stayed together the entire afternoon. Benny saved his suitcase, and I saved his travel bag. A lot of people from the transport administration helped me. Otto Mändl and Peter came too and stayed until evening. Daddy came and we took him to the Sudeten barracks, where he's very badly accommodated. The next day we went to the Genie barracks, and he'll eventually be moved to the tubercular ward. He's extremely satisfied in Theresienstadt. He feels well and is happy to be with us. He's not hungry and so is lacking nothing. We found his sleeping bag and his second bag.

SEPTEMBER 15, THURSDAY: Benny, Peter, and I visit Eva every evening. It's almost like Prague again. Once we came home at 11:30 P.M. and a ghetto guard stopped us near the citadel. There was a huge row. He wanted to report us and said something about Poland. We were out of our minds with fear. Benny tried everything, but he wouldn't budge. I went home. Mommy was waiting for me at the door. She was horribly upset. Just today there was a notice in the newspaper saying that nobody is allowed on the street after 9 P.M. After 12 A.M. they have orders to shoot. I calmed her down but was upset myself. Benny visited in the morning. Everything's settled—the report was revoked. The next few nights I went to the Hamburg.

Eva's parents and Vera have been sent to Poland. It was horrible. Nobody agreed with Eva's decision to stay here alone. Peter's parents came, and a week later they were put into a transport. Peter volunteered to go with them, and now the group consists of just Eva, Benny, and me.

The food situation has improved lately. I'm supplying the whole family. It's not always easy, but it works, and I'm happy about it. Mommy and I get at least triple, sometimes even quadruple portions at lunch for a few vegetables from meal duty. Every afternoon I go to the Viktoria Hotel to fetch food for the watchdog. Sometimes they give me milk or food left over from lunch. I gladly take both, and the three of us make dinner from it. We have a few vegetables here and there, so if we divide it well, there's enough food for dinner. We're getting a large ration of potatoes, flour, and margarine lately.

There's enough bread now too. It seems that nothing's changed at all politically. We're all preparing to spend the winter here.

Mama, Lotte, and the children arrived from Prague on the fifteenth. We walked with them from Bohušovice to the sluice. They didn't let us in Bohušovice but with some effort, we got in anyway. We spent all day with them. Thank God nothing happened to their luggage. It's the first transport where they could get everything right away. People were ordered to take as little as possible. They let some unimportant person search the suitcases. They were very well informed. They spent a few days on the floor in the blockhouse. They were accommodated very poorly and then moved into the Hamburg. In return for some tomatoes I was able to get them into the blockhouses.

Mommy is very ill. One day she had a fever of over 104°F and horrible diarrhea. Almost everybody has that here. It's a kind of dysentery and mainly weakens the heart. When she got better, I didn't save any of the rations anymore. I cooked a hearty lunch and dinner at Eva's. Later I made sure she always got some milk. Thank God it's better now. I'm getting food from the Magdeburg meals as well. Besides that, I take Mama and Eva some vegetables every day. I've had more confidence lately. I've been successfully smuggling the most unbelievable things. Some marvelous mattresses, for instance. There's a supply area nobody knows about. It's like sleeping on a feather bed for me and Mommy. I'm still trading the few vegetables I have for margarine, shoes, and other things. Meal duty's running smoothly. We have three to four lunches a day. Then I get half a bucket of normal food for the dog in the Magdeburg, and in the Viktoria either normal food, which is of course excellent, or milk.

■   ■   ■

OCTOBER 8, WEDNESDAY: Shops have opened. All Theresienstadt is laughing. The displays are full of the most gorgeous things: groceries, clothes, shoes, paper, household utensils, perfumes, and finery. Everything they took from everybody else is on exhibit here. People are saying that Germans are coming to visit. A few days later we found out that the things on display really were for sale. In fact, they're for workers with points. Mommy got some very soon, and then later so did I. Of course the entire purchase turned out to be a horrible fraud. You've got to take whatever they give you. People who have connections get more and decent things. People who don't have connections get turnip juice, ginger powder, and other such nonsense. Even without connections you can get nice clothes. Contraband items like thermoses, canteens, and hot plates, which were always taken from stolen suitcases in the transports are now on display and can be purchased. What a farce!

I'm with Mama every day. She's terribly afraid of the Poland transport. She wasn't put in the first one and was assured that the danger of being in one might indeed be over. Work is the same as usual, except that I have to play maid for Kraus and have lots to do. But even that has advantages. Sometimes I even get white bread at the Viktoria Hotel. Imagine having pureed peas, marrow bones, and other things like that. Mommy's job is hideous. If only I could get her something else. But that's terribly difficult—you have to have connections, and we have none at all. Daddy wasn't allowed out of the barracks for a while. He had to stay put because of the Poland transport. Poland transports are leaving with Germans from the Reich, who were never considered for them before. But since the mortality rate was so high, an order came that Germans between the ages of sixty-five and ninety had to go if they made it alive to Bohušovice. It's dreadful to witness this.

The situation has improved in terms of freedom and rations on the one hand, but on the other, you can't bear to look inside the blockhouses for all the dirt and illness. There are people with dysentery lying one on top of the other, corpses squeezed together with half corpses for days at a time, mattresses that are soaked through and can't be changed so you find worms underneath them. All this should be filmed and sent overseas! Nobody could possibly imagine it.

I visit Eva every evening. She's moved to her grandmother's, and Eva, Benny, and I sit on the veranda every evening. I'm so happy to have them.

OCTOBER 15, THURSDAY: I've been put in jail and am alone in a cell. It's a week today, and I still can't grasp it. It's so unbelievable and implausible that were it not for the terrible fact that Benny is in jail because of me, I'd think it was all a bad dream. Here's how it happened: I wasn't at Kraus's anymore. I had to go to the pasture with the sheep. I was unhappy because first, I had to give up my various sources of income, and second, I don't like to lie around on the grass. I prefer a normal job. I've told that to everybody, including Wilda. I suspect Wilda's the one that got me into this mess, but his intentions were good. He didn't want me to be Kraus's maid. In short, within a week, I was given my old job again.

Meanwhile, though, the pasture had its advantages. Even more than I had while working for Kraus. So I was happy nonetheless. An Aryan and his wife and two of their children worked in the pasture we went to. They were very nice to me from the start. By the second day the man brought me bread and sausage and discussed politics with me. It was very interesting. The next day he brought me an even bigger piece of sausage, which I took home, and a small jar of real honey. I was in heaven. The next day I got a couple of pounds of hulled oats, twenty cigarettes, and a cigar and matches from him. He wanted absolutely nothing for it. Supposedly he earned enough from others and was happy to do it for Daddy and Mommy.

I brought him some of our linen. The next day I didn't go to the pasture. Another day I came back again during the noon break. He was there, but he was with a stranger and probably didn't dare to do anything in front of her. Mimi came in the afternoon with a message from the Aryan. I had to go to the pasture because he had some things for me and didn't want to take them back home a second time. I told Kraus I was going to fetch the sheep and got a couple of pounds of sausage and fat, twelve onions, two heads of garlic, one cigar, ten cigarettes, and candy.

On the way home I got scared and didn't know where to put them. Nothing came to mind, and anyway, we've never been inspected when we were with the animals. I hid the cigarettes in my bra and the fat in the back of my coat where it's held by a belt.

The first policeman was nice. Silly goose that I am. How could I have been afraid? Then the garden. A policeman yelled, "Stop! Come here, young lady. What have you got in your bread bag?" "I've got to get to the sheep!" I answered. And he said, "It doesn't matter. Let them run!"

I didn't care about anything. Him: "Ah, sausage, where did you get it? And a cigar and an onion?" The smith was standing close by. I gave him an imploring look, but he couldn't do anything. The policeman: "Open up your coat!" He looked at the package. Me: "There's only some bread and butter in there."

Him: "Where's the money?" Me: "I don't have any money." Him: "Well, we'll get it out of you. And where did you get the other things?" Me: "The sausage is from the last transport, I found the cigar, and the onions are from the garden." Him again: "Well, we'll get it out of you."

He also searched the other two girls, Doris Schimmerling and Hanka Seltzer, but didn't find anything on them: "You two can go. You come with me!" Good God, the cigarettes in my bra! I walked down an endless path and kept repeating to myself: "It's nothing bad; I brought some food to last the day in the pasture. We didn't want to slice up the sausage, the onion came from a friend in the garden, and I found the cigar on the street."

Everybody was looking at me the whole way. I calmly waved to friends. Nothing's going to happen. But the cigarettes! Finally I was able to stick my hand under my shirt and push them out. Don't turn around. They're out. Thank God, nothing more can happen to me now. I was taken to the officers' headquarters.

All the policemen obviously felt sorry for me. I was taken to be interrogated. They screamed at me terribly. I was completely calm. I had to unpack everything and also had about ten slices of bread with me from the Viktoria Hotel. That was good! They didn't even look at the fat, just the sausage, the onion, and the cigar. They didn't believe me. "Who did you get the sausage from?" "From the last transport." "From whom?" All of a sudden the name Klein came to mind. I don't know why. I wonder if they even exist. I don't care. The Kleins are in Poland by now. "The onions?" "From the boys in the garden." "For heaven's sake, from whom?" They played with a revolver and threatened to shoot me. "Benny Grünberger." That was the biggest mistake I could possibly have made. They immediately wrote

ABOVE: Antonia Mändl, Eva's mother. Neither of Eva's parents survived the war.

BELOW: Eva's father, Arnost Mändl. He received Austria's highest gold medal of honor for courage in World War I. Mr. Mändl's status as a war hero could not keep him or his family out of Theresienstadt.

ABOVE: Eva Mändl before the war.

RIGHT: The Mändl house in Saaz.

TOP: Eva's fiancé, Richard, second from the left, poses for a picture with his fellow soldiers in the Czech division of the British Army.

BELOW: Eva and friends at a swimming area on the outskirts of Prague that was off-limits to Jews. Eva is in the front right corner; next to her is Vera Glauber, then Eva Glauber.

LEFT: Happier days: Eva and friends skiing in the Czech mountains. Eva is at far right, her friend Käthe on the left. The man in the middle is unidentified.

BELOW: Ballroom dancing lessons in Saaz around 1936. Eva, second girl from the right, is fifteen.

down where he lives. The same for Doris and Hanka. Benny gave me some onions a week ago. He'll say they're from Kurzawe and somehow manage to talk his way out of it. I'm not worried about him. "Where did you get the cigar?" "I found it on the street two days ago. I didn't know what to do with it and thought it might make somebody happy. But I haven't found anybody yet."

Him: "Take her to the Dresden barracks!" I walked with a guard through Theresienstadt and met acquaintances along the way again. They were all bewildered, but somehow it's got to be cleared up. "I'm not allowed to go home?" I asked. "No!" There were no more cigarettes on the spot where I lost them. I saw Benny's face at the window of the guards' room in the Dresden. He moved his lips in the same way over and over. "Transport!" "Transport!" What does he mean by that? I looked at him, bewildered, unable to say a word. Finally it occurred to me. "The sausage came from the transport." Good! They inspected my pockets and found a note with the Aryan's signature and an exact description of everything he gave me. For God's sake, did they notice anything? The policeman seemed decent. He scolded me for being so clumsy. "May I keep the note for toilet paper?" "No. You'll be given some." Where did the note go? I was taken to a cell.

A tall blond woman took me to a cell. I expected her to do a complete body search, but nothing happened. I was to spend three days in darkness with nothing to eat. How can I speak to Benny? After five minutes I hammered on the door. The blond woman came. "May I go to the toilet? I have diarrhea." "Yes, as an exception, but you're only allowed to go three times a day. Otherwise you use the bucket." A policeman walked with her. I didn't see any sign of Benny.

On the way back a ghetto guard whispered, "The gentleman said to tell you that the sausage is from the transport and the onions are from Bischitzki." Benny's outrageous. How did he know everything already? Great. He's going to Wilda. He'll say he got the onions from Wilda. The worst part so far are the Kleins. Nobody's heard of them. Will they interrogate my parents too?

I was in a small dark cell, utterly alone with my thoughts. It was supposed to last for three days. It could drive a person crazy. After a while I pounded on the door again. The policeman was very decent, and I had to talk to somebody. "Can I have my coat, please? I have three pieces of candy in it." "But miss, the coat must be in there with you. It isn't out here." "Oh, yes, it's so dark in here. I'm so sorry. Thank you." And then I was alone again.

I opened the window a little. It had thick iron bars, and behind them there was a hall with all sorts of things, then more bars, and then the Dresden barracks yard. I walked back and forth. Can you turn thoughts off? In this situation it's impossible. Tomorrow I'm going to be interrogated again. I'm horribly tired. I was given my things: a blanket, sweatpants, toilet articles. Who brought them? A boy came with them. Benny's fabulous. They must know about everything at home. They'll be very upset. Poor Mommy!

I fell asleep and was awakened suddenly. Everybody went out to the toilet and washroom. There were a few girls outside, Doris and Hanka among them. "It's good that you're here. I've got something to tell you both." Her: "Pst, pst." A policeman came to take us across the yard and to the toilet. "Tell Mommy she shouldn't worry." "But we're in jail too," she said. "Heavens, in jail because of me! Impossible! What about your family? They'll be furious with me." "Benny's in jail too, in the Sudeten barracks."

I felt as if I was going to faint. It was like a bomb. For God's sake, what was I doing giving his name like that? It can't be. He's completely innocent.

The girls didn't make a big deal out of it and haven't blamed me at all. I had to give their names. After all, we had our identity cards with us. But I didn't have to give Benny's name.

I slept very little that night. I was taken to the washroom in the morning. God, if only they'd let Benny and the girls out.

A policeman escorted us to the officers' headquarters to be interrogated in the morning. We discussed everything quickly beforehand. In any case, they don't know anything. I alone was interrogated for a long time, but they only wrote up a short report. They screamed a lot at me again. I repeated what I'd said the night before. Do any Kleins even exist? Or maybe they're still here and could get into trouble. If only I knew what's happening with Benny.

Then the three of us were led back to the Dresden again. I had three days of darkness and no food. Hanka and Doris were released. Certainly Benny was released too. Why don't my parents come? I gave Hanka a message for them to find out if the Kleins do or do not exist but haven't heard anything. I'm sure they're very upset. My parents were finally there when we were taken out at noon again. They were very pale and upset. Benny's still in jail. There are twelve Kleins.

■   ■   ■

What can I do the whole day? It wouldn't be so bad if it weren't so terribly dark. I got some sleeping powder. I take it day and night and sleep almost continuously. Otherwise you could go crazy.

A policeman took us all to the toilet and washroom at nine in the morning. My parents come to the window every day. They were at Edelstein's. Wilda went to Clausen. Everything possible is being attempted from every angle. But they shouldn't do it for me. They should devote their energy to Benny, who's completely innocent. Eva's trying to help Benny. But Wilda should do something for him.

We get coffee in the morning, lunch at noon, and then dinner. We're let out at two o'clock and at eight o'clock. Doris visits me every day. She's very good and brings me food from the Hannover barracks. It comes from Mimi. Supposedly Benny's being well taken care of too.

Everybody thinks we'll both be sent to Poland. My parents absolutely want to go with me. I'm trying to talk them into letting us go there alone. Eva wants to go too. I wrote Benny a letter, but I don't know if he received it. The day is endless. I read, mend socks. There's no clock and time slowly creeps by. Almost all the policemen are very decent.

Most of the people locked up here are young. Mostly for having contact with Aryans. A half-Jewish woman from Bohušovice is in here for having contact with Jews. She has four children. Ten thousand people have to go to Poland. Nothing can protect us anymore, neither the AK nor anything else, only the ghetto guards. Six thousand old people and four thousand young people have to go.

Our supervisor's terrible. She's there only for the guards, not for us. She won't give us anything but wants to take everything we have. And yet she's got everything she needs and then some. Grandma Gibian went with the very first transport. She came to the window to say good-bye. Everybody's terribly on edge.

Two people have been released: a young girl and a woman. The next day they were sent to Poland. Nobody's released without going to Poland. I'm completely prepared for it and convinced I'll be going too. My poor parents! They went to Edelstein once more and came back relieved. They saw it in black and white. I'm going to be released, without Poland, and Benny supposedly as well. Our supervisor also told me I was going home either today or tomorrow. But it was neither today nor tomorrow. I didn't make a big deal out of it. My parents are unhappy. They and Mama come to visit me almost every day.

OCTOBER 18, SUNDAY: Another two women from here are in the transport. Mommy came. Benny's in the transport too. She stood at the window the whole day and begged me not to do anything stupid. And I begged her again to let me go with him. I've never cried so much in my entire life. It's simply dreadful. I can't take it. It's impossible that they'll just send him away. Why don't they send me away? Can't I go in his place? I absolutely have to do something so that he gets out, and if I can't, I want to go with him, no matter what. My parents are very unhappy. They cried the whole day. They're completely at a loss and in despair. What should I do? Should I listen to my parents? It's awful to think of going on living here. But to bring disaster upon my parents? They won't let me go alone and will volunteer to go. That would be horrible for them both. The transport is leaving tomorrow. When will they let him go? Eva's grandmother and Benny's grandmother went. Eva spent the entire day at the citadel packing and wasn't able to say good-bye to either of them. Benny's leaving on the twenty-second.

OCTOBER 21, WEDNESDAY: Benny was released on Tuesday. He visited me that afternoon in my cell. He was completely calm, made nothing of it. He even consoled me. But can you console anybody in a situation like this? He said that what I did, giving his name, was completely natural. That when a person's in trouble, they think of their best friend. He doesn't want me to go with him or Eva to volunteer. O.K. [a friend of Benny's] behaved fabulously. He gave him all his rations and others are giving him whatever they can.

OCTOBER 22, THURSDAY: I stood at the window the entire afternoon. I feel I've aged years. Benny finally came. I wanted to say so much to him, and then once he was there, I couldn't even open my mouth. I just gave him a note. He keeps consoling me. I don't want to live anymore. This is no life. He said he can't leave in peace with me like this. I had to promise not to do anything stupid. I couldn't think at all. All I could do was cry. I was completely empty. Good-bye until Prague and much, much luck.

OCTOBER 23, FRIDAY–NOVEMBER 7, SATURDAY: I'm taking sleeping powder and can only sleep and cry and cry again and sleep again. It has all been so unbelievable and so terrible. It hurt to think. It was like a wound that kept splitting open. Then I became completely apathetic. Lots of people came, but I was incapable of doing anything. I couldn't speak, and then I wasn't even able to cry anymore. I didn't want to live. That was the only thing I could think of. The policemen and everybody were very decent. I think I must have changed a lot. I've become either hysterical or terribly selfish or a bit of both. I couldn't eat and couldn't work. Eva visited me every day. The poor thing is all alone now. Two thousand old people are in the transport, but they didn't have enough, so at the last moment they called up a thousand young people. Lots of AK and people who previously had been one hundred percent protected were in it. Löwenstein made that happen. Around twenty people were put into jail. It has to do with money. A report was filed from Vienna. Seven people, including Oli and Lotte, were put into a small cell. Around sixty people who weren't put into the transport or into the sluice went home. The men went to the local headquarters, and the women came here. Some of them were brought here on stretchers.

I cry a lot, but mostly only when it gets dark. Otherwise I'm calm, just somewhat more serious and sadder than the others. And yet the others have at least as much to worry about. Oli, who's the soul of the jail, has four children. Her Aryan husband died, and she's locked up in here. She doesn't belong in the ghetto at all. Her children are in Bohušovice. One of them is even said to have died. She doesn't know, but she's always in a good mood. Lotte has an Aryan husband in Prague whom she's divorced from and is here with her small child. She's doing time because her brother's wife was captured in Bohušovice. Her mother had to go to Poland. The child is sick and utterly alone. She'll probably go to Poland with the next transport.

If I'm released without having to go to Poland, which everyone is working on, what kind of life will I have? Can I walk around Theresienstadt in a normal way without everybody looking at me askance? Can I ever face Benny's parents and Danny again? Especially when he was so looking forward to seeing them. He arranged with Edelstein that they'd be secure here.

The people in the last transport were only allowed to take one suitcase weighing thirty pounds and no sleeping bags. The fifth transport was postponed, because they had no people left for it. Over seventy women stayed here for five days. Each cell was led out individually, then children from the Protectorate. On the fifth day they suddenly released anyone left behind. There are four of us in a cell. Hanka has gorgeous blond hair and lice. A whole headful. She had to wash her head with petroleum. Lotte looks for more to give her every day. There are more than enough bugs and fleas here. I don't have any for the time being, but if I did, I wouldn't care. Nothing can upset me anymore. If it weren't the worst thing for my parents to go to Poland, I'd volunteer immediately for the next transport. We're not allowed to turn the lights on after 6 P.M. because of the 150 people here, and the barracks have a 6 P.M. curfew. Nobody was allowed on the streets on Sunday and Monday except with a pass. The punishment lasted from Thursday to Monday. My parents visit me every day. Mama, Jarka Pollak, Doris, and Mimi, who's very good, often visit too. It feels good to see there are still people who don't judge me and who understand my point of view.

The Aryan who gave me the things is horrible. He tells everybody how much he'd like to help me, that he'd give everything he has, money and all he owns, to get me out. But he's talking so much and to so many people that he'll create a disaster for himself and cause me even more harm. Supposedly I'm getting out on November 8. Now all of a sudden he's afraid I'll denounce him. Our supervisor doesn't take care of us at all. She's heartless and selfish through and through and doesn't even try to hide it.

She's especially rough on the old women, so much so that it's scandalous. She only cares about her clothes and her comfort. We have water all day and cook tea for ourselves sometimes.

NOVEMBER 8, SATURDAY: Today's the eighth, and I'm sitting and waiting. Will they release me? I don't know whether I should be glad or not. It'll be terrible out there. What will all my friends say? Will I be fired from the farm? It'll be difficult to get to Wilda. But my parents are so happy. I don't want to take their joy away. It isn't so awful here. Maybe I'll never be let out. I don't care.

NOVEMBER 18, WEDNESDAY: I've been home now for over a week. The week just flew by. It felt like a single day in jail. Everything worked out better than I'd imagined. Everybody, without exception, was very kind to me. I was released at noon. Daddy picked me up, and on the way we met Mommy. My parents are very happy. Everybody in the room I had so feared to enter has shown such kindness. I visited Edelstein, Klaber, and Schliesser with Daddy in the afternoon. I spoke with Edelstein. Later I went to the Družstvo [Cooperative]. Wilda wasn't there. Eva's in the hospital. She was terribly glad to see me. She isn't doing too well. Mama was terribly sweet too. I spoke to Tonda and Wilda on Monday at the Družstvo. Tonda scolded me. Of course he's completely right. Wilda didn't scold me at all. "You've certainly repented enough already. Just go back to work tending the sheep." That's wonderful. I was afraid I'd have to look for a new job. People stopped me everywhere on the street. All my friends greeted and congratulated me. I'd like to know what for. My stupidity? The street makes my head spin. There are so many people everywhere. It's so terribly crowded everywhere. Am I at all normal anymore? I feel that everybody on the street can tell

st come out of jail. Don't they notice anything? It's as if
turned from a long journey. Everything's so unfamiliar. It
s as though I'd been gone not a month but at least a year.
It's been an endlessly long time. I feel insecure and have lost
my self-confidence. I'm shy and afraid of people. I'm afraid of
everything. I think about Benny day and night. The consequences one word had. I was welcomed very kindly by the
Krauses. The girls behaved fabulously. I'm working again, and
everything is the same as usual. Nothing's changed. I'm talking again and slowly getting used to things. But at night I can't
sleep. Everything's much worse than during the day.

The Aryan wrote me two long letters and sent a Jew to give me
an apple and some margarine. I wrote him he should stop. It's
not worth getting another person thrown into jail for it. I'm
working for Kraus again. I deliver milk in the morning. They're
especially nice at the Viktoria. I spoke to them even in front of
the SS. O.K. had been working there before I got there. I would
like to have spoken with him once. Zeki has his position now,
and he's very good to work with. I fetch food for the dog every
day at noon. The dog barely gets a quarter of it, but it's more
than enough. So we're all well provided for again. The geese get
a kettle of cooked potatoes every day, and naturally we take
some of that too. It's a lot of work, but it's worth it.

I visit the girls in the Dresden barracks every day. It's where I
feel best. It's quiet, and there isn't such a bustle. I go into the
cell almost every time. After all, I know all the policemen. I
come home at five. Daddy's with us all the time, and we eat
together. Jarka picks me up at 6:45, and we visit Eva. She's
been doing very badly for two days now. She's got a fever of
over 100°F and is bleeding day and night. It's terrible. The
poor thing has nobody besides me, and she's very, very sick.

Basically I've taken Benny away from her. She needed him more than anybody and yet she's modest, needs nothing, and is just happy when somebody comes to visit her.

DECEMBER 2, WEDNESDAY: Life goes on. Everything goes on. If somebody had told me that a month ago, I wouldn't have thought it possible. A transport came from Prague. I was very upset two days before it. If the Grünbergers were to come, it would be terrible. How would I tell them? What would my parents say if they came here with the absolute certainty I was here, and somebody told them I had to go to Poland because of a terrible mistake? I couldn't see the transport even though I tried. I can't get out of Theresienstadt, and it's impossible to find anybody here. Finally I got to see the lists. The Grünbergers didn't come, but the Justitzes, Eva's relatives, did. I found out from them that the Grünbergers were in the transport but escaped to Slovakia the night before. Nobody knows whether they were successful.

It's really a terrible thing to do to Benny, just abandoning him like that, especially when he could fall into the hands of the Germans at any moment. Maybe it's lucky he knows nothing; otherwise he'd have been very upset. A friend from Slovakia will give them some more help. I don't quite understand it all, whether it's worth it, especially since they were informed that it isn't so bad here and that they would most likely be safe from Poland.

Eva's still in the hospital. She isn't doing well. The last few days she was in great pain again. It's a kidney infection. I visit her every evening with Jarka. He's well behaved and kindhearted. Every Friday there's a get-together in the Magdeburg barracks. Three boys have a beautiful room. One of them is in our group.

There's singing and guitar playing. There are always about fifteen people around. Egon's very nice, and the other two have their girls there too. I got a pass for after eight from them.

At work they say one moment that the animals are going to be sold, and then that they won't. I'd be happy if everything stayed as is. Sure, it's hard work, peeling potatoes the whole day, carrying them around in baskets, washing, and removing manure from animals' pens . . . but still, I get four to six pounds of cooked potatoes, which we eat at lunch and in the evening, and sometimes even in the morning and afternoon. The three of us live off that. And then there's vegetables sometimes. Daddy's stomach has been bothering him lately. I still often go to the Dresden barracks and usually take something for them. Transports to Poland have been suspended for the time being. Theresienstadt is going through a cultural upswing. Every night there's a cabaret. Sometimes I go, and the best part is a performance of *The Bartered Bride* [Bedřich Smetana's opera], which is supposed to be very good. There's a piano and a harmonium, and we have excellent artists here.

DECEMBER 9, WEDNESDAY: As of today I'll have been home for an entire month. It's gone by incredibly fast. I haven't changed outwardly to people who don't know me well, but I know that I'm different. I've become phlegmatic. I don't care about anything at all. No matter what happened, it would leave me cold. Every evening I go to see Eva with Jarka. I go with him even though he never says or does anything about it. Aside from that, I often go to the Magdeburg barracks, and Egon and I talk. But it's all so superficial. I wander around the pasture, without any Aryan contact, of course. I haven't heard anything more from my Aryan since then. We're back to living on just potatoes. Daddy's on a special diet and is always hungry. I take something to Eva every day as well, so now we're a family of four. I'm glad it works. Eva still has a fever all the time. Everybody has lots of work here, everybody's overworked, so there's no time to think about anything. Two transports from Pardubitz have arrived. Theresienstadt is overcrowded, and there are two great dangers: vermin, which increase visibly by the day, and typhoid. There's a good deal of typhoid going around lately, and lots of people, even young people, are dying from it. Nothing's changed politically. As usual, "everything's fine, we'll be going home soon." It's always the same, and it's too little. We hear bits and pieces of information: either they're wonderful, and then we find out they're not true, or they're from the newspaper and meaningless, and have no influence. Nothing is happening, nothing at all. At least we don't know of anything.

DECEMBER 10, THURSDAY: A year ago today we were in the transport. It's been a long year. Nobody could have imagined we'd still be here, and maybe we'll still be here a year from now. We're alive, and life goes on, eating and sleeping, talking with one another, even laughing occasionally, and sometimes it even resembles normal life here. We don't even notice anymore; that's how used to it we've become. This week the goats, the kids, and a hundred sheep were sold. It's certain that many of us will be let go of. I'll probably stay.

The Aryan sent me someone again. He wants me to drop him a line and tell him how I'm doing. I just want to be very, very careful. Sometimes I walk through the pasture, near the crematoriums.[1] Once I was inside. It's like a huge factory for

---

[1] Theresienstadt was not an extermination camp. The crematorium was used to cremate people who had died of illness or had been executed.

burning people, four ovens day and night. You can see the corpses slowly burning, only the bones remain, and then they crumble.

Besides the kidney problem, Eva's been diagnosed with scarlet fever, now that it's nearly over, and in addition she has jaundice, the fashionable illness around here. So the fever wasn't from the kidneys. I visit her daily with Jarka. I can't feel anything intensely anymore, neither joy nor sorrow. Nothing touches me. I often go to the Dresden barracks and to see Egon too. I saw *The Bartered Bride* and was thoroughly inspired. It makes you forget everything. Every day between fifteen and twenty geese are slaughtered. I'm only able to bring raw potatoes home now, and it's extremely difficult to find a place to cook them.

Daddy has been promised a job in the warehouse. That would be wonderful. Having to worry about every meal is terrible. Neither Mommy nor I have time to cook, and Daddy's hungry at lunch and dinner. Mommy looks a bit better, Daddy too, and even I've put on some weight. Many people are getting packages. If only we could notify our people in Prague that they're allowed to send us things! Mama's with us every day; she's quite unhappy with Lotte and the children and working more than she should.

DECEMBER 30, WEDNESDAY: I have two friends now, Jarka and Egon. Both are very decent and both have their faults. I can't claim to feel particularly happy about it. I'm amused, that's all. Jarka's a year younger than me. Egon's my age. I visit Eva every day with Jarka, and he brings us both bread. Eva's still sick, she has a fever all the time, and they suspect typhus. She had diarrhea, and no doctor seems able to figure out what's wrong. I usually go to see Egon from the Dresden. There's usually a nice group of people in the Magdeburg. Christmas Eve passed without much of a celebration. I was in the Dresden barracks, where there was some drinking, then went to the Magdeburg with Doris for a while. We were home by ten.

I've received a package from my Aryan. I don't know what to do: on the one hand, I'd like to see him—it isn't right that he sends me and Eva things for free, and I'd really like to send him to Prague, but the people who bring me the things strongly advise me against it, because he's very careless and tells everything to total strangers. When he heard I had a sick friend, he sent her honey, butter, and fruit. Isn't that wonderful! Up to now he's sent me three hundred cigarettes, two pounds of honey, eight pounds of flour, pastries, two pounds of margarine, two pounds of smoked meat, and saccharin. If I were to tell anyone about it, it would sound like a fairy tale. The most wonderful things come to my room with no risk to me and at no cost. It's terribly cold in the pasture. Sometimes we warm ourselves in the crematorium. Daddy's been in a bad mood lately. He's hungry all the time. He hasn't visited us for several days.

I'm with Mama every day. The children [Lotte's] are a nuisance. Jana looks terrible, and she doesn't get along with the other children in the nursery.

1943

JANUARY 10, WEDNESDAY: I'm sick. I've got strep throat. It's not serious, I can walk around, but I don't go to work. Everything can be taken care of at home. New Year's Eve was quite nice. There was a large gathering in the Magdeburg, mostly people we didn't know. Doris was there too. It was fine for an evening, but the people weren't exactly to my taste. Most of the people there had always been well off, and even here they're not suffering. They don't care about anything, and they have no interest and no worries. Totally superficial. Some people played the harmonica, others guitar and mandolin. There was dancing, a show, and food. Egon was by far the nicest person there. It was lively until around three in the morning. Then little by little everyone fell asleep. I couldn't sleep and talked with Egon. It wasn't good company for Doris. A sixteen-year-old girl doesn't fit in there. Nothing bad happened, but I had an unpleasant feeling because she came there with me. I didn't want to take her, but she wanted to go so badly, and she had her mother's permission. We came home at half past five in the morning. Not sleepy the whole day.

Another ten thousand people are supposed to go to Poland, half of them from the Protectorate. Will I be one of them? Nobody knows my fears. Hanka and Lotte have been let out of jail. Lotte's in the Poland transport. I'm feeling horrendously miserable again. Everything looks so wretched. The whole world is bad, I'm bad, Theresienstadt has made me bad. Will I ever be fit for normal life again? You simply can't get by here any other way. Lots of people here have it easier than me. I have to fight hard for everything. Daddy's in a bad mood. He didn't get the job in the warehouse, and he's angry at the whole world. Yet every night he gets plenty of food from us. They've started inspections again, but for now only in the blocks. I'm really scared about the four hundred cigarettes. I've sewn them into a mattress. I hope it works. I was interrogated about the Hanka business. Mama's with us every day. She's such a fine person, and I like her so much because she isn't bad like all the others. She's even too good and spoils the children. She takes her work too seriously and torments herself and treats each patient like her own child. She has trouble fitting in here. She takes everything too tragically, especially the dirt and the cramped quarters.

The dirt and the vermin are getting more and more unbearable. We're squeezed together even more, and there are more fleas, bedbugs, and lice every day. Under the circumstances it's absolutely impossible to fight it, with people lying one on top of the other. Especially in the blocks where they're housed in such inhuman conditions. The lice in people's hair and clothes has gotten terrifyingly out of hand.

It's January, and officially we're still not allowed to start heating. But in nearly all the barracks they're doing it anyway. In the blocks people are slowly freezing to death, especially in the attic, where there's no way the heat can reach them. People have been found frozen to death at temperatures of 4 degrees below zero. What's the outcome? Many people have to be housed in the barracks, where they're crammed together even more. The normal reaction to this of course is more transports to Poland, as terrible as that sounds, but Poland couldn't be worse than here in the attic. They can't do more than freeze to death in Poland. On the other hand, we have the nightly cabaret, dances, a coffeehouse with excellent music, and apartments with real couches, all at the Magdeburg barracks, where I go every day.

But I can never forget the misery. There's no place where I can feel a hundred percent at ease. Eva is my only girlfriend. She's still doing badly. Last week she suddenly had a fever of over 104°F for several days. It was dreadful to see her wasting away. Now she's doing a bit better. If only she'd get well. But she's so patient and never complains, and there's no one far and wide she's closer to. Her relatives don't take care of her at all. If she needs anything, she always tells me. I'd gladly do anything for her, but then again, I feel awful when I think of her parents. God only knows where they are, when she'll see them again, and now she only has me, an inexperienced young thing, when she so desperately needs her mother.

Politically the situation doesn't seem to have changed at all. We hear all sorts of rumors, but they're probably nonsense and have so little influence on what happens. When are we going home? That's the question in Theresienstadt. It sounds so beautiful, but what if the war did come to an end? What would things be like? What would a victory look like? It's very, very improbable, even impossible that we could simply start over where we left off. Where will we go anyway? Where is our home? What's going to happen to us after the war? Who knows what's going on with Richard, whether he even thinks about me anymore. For me he means the future, but will he think that way too? It's been so long. I'd rather not stay in Europe. I want to go far away from here. Europe will be horrible after the war. And even if it remains intact, who can guarantee that in twenty years my children won't have the same misfortune I've had? I don't want that no matter what. I don't want to go to Palestine. Maybe to America. Maybe people are more reasonable there and not so shortsighted and won't allow themselves to be swayed as they do here, but then, they aren't all that likable either.

Many people receive packages here, especially the people who smuggle out letters. I don't, and we don't receive any packages. The Aryan sent me a whole liverwurst for New Year's, but since then I haven't heard anything from him. Lotte's just written to her boyfriend to go to Mr. Glaser, too, so they can get in touch. If the Glasers sent our things, we would be taken care of for a while. Only certain special people are officially allowed to write, and even then, it's uncertain whether the messages get there.

Mommy's work is very difficult. She's often on night duty. If only she could get another job, but that's entirely out of the question. Things were much worse a year ago than they are now. If anyone had told us then that we'd still be here in a year, we'd never have imagined we could make it. . . . Anyway, it has improved here somewhat. Where will we be a year from now?

JANUARY 12, TUESDAY: Celebrated Mommy's birthday. She got a cake and ham for supper. Hopefully her next birthday will be better, hopefully she'll have a better year, hopefully she'll be happy.

JANUARY 27, WEDNESDAY: Transports, transports, nothing but transports to Poland. The first two full of mandatory deportations; I'm positive I'll be included. People have been forced to go for the tiniest blunders and for meaningless things. Matters that were resolved long ago suddenly turn into deportations. It's simply unbelievable, inconceivable, and an amazing stroke of luck that I'm not in the transport. Of course it's not out of the question I'll be forced to go, because nobody is safe anymore, but if I do go, then it can hardly be called a deportation anymore.

In the meantime some new people have arrived. An average of five hundred of them went again, but they still take people from the old transports, and the new children from the Protectorate stay here. That's not fair.

JANUARY 29, FRIDAY: There are big changes in the ghetto. A new council of elders. Epstein from Berlin is the Jewish elder, Löwenstein from Vienna his deputy; Edelstein is third in command. That will probably have repercussions. In any case a lot more people from the Protectorate will be leaving than before.

FEBRUARY 3, WEDNESDAY: The new council of elders hasn't made any changes yet. Löwenstein has been replaced by Murmelstein, an even bigger swine. Mandler has driven with Fiedler from Prague, Weidmann with his family of sixteen. Mandler got beaten up, to the delight of the entire ghetto. For the moment there are no more transports to Poland or any worker transports or the possibility that Edelstein is leaving and building a new ghetto somewhere else.

According to German reports, the Russians have launched a huge offensive on the Russian front. The Germans were surrounded at Stalingrad and forced to surrender. The Russians are advancing on all fronts. Things are going well in Africa too.

The English have taken Tripoli, and there's hope that the war will end there soon. We're supposedly protected from the transports as long as we're working the land. Mommy was on duty in the typhoid unit for a few days. It was terrible, and she's glad she's back in the Hamburg. It's frightening how fast typhoid spreads. It's a huge danger. Thank God they're mostly light cases. We're with Mama every day again. The children keep acting up, and sometimes Mama complains. They get lots of packages, both officially and unofficially, and have a little of everything. I always get something too. Got something from my Aryan again. Flour and margarine, sugar, fat, syrup, and other things. He wrote a long letter saying he would always take care of me as long as it was within his power and he didn't want a thing in return. And if I have to go to Poland, he has even offered to hide me and will let me stay with him until the war ends. Isn't that unbelievable?

I can take enough potatoes home, and we're glad to have them even if they're bad. I've gained weight, and I don't want to get too fat. Mommy looks good too, better than in a long while. Daddy could eat from morning till evening. Thank God we always have something to give him. Eva's home. She's got a nice room with lots of young girls who cook all day. The boys always take them something to eat, smuggling in bulk even by the ghetto guards. Every transport they take entire suitcases, and they claim that the ghetto guard doesn't smuggle. Löwenstein wants to bring military order into the ghetto and is strictly enforcing it.

The bakery is set up. Jarka's in the children's kitchen. He's good at that kind of thing, even though he's often unpleasant. I'm with Egon almost every night. One of the men from his room had to go to Poland, and a nice fellow came in his place, with an even nicer wife. I get along with Egon fabulously. It's friendship with a bit of flirting here and there. He's helping me to get over the horrible episode with Benny.

FEBRUARY 11, THURSDAY: I'm sick and in bed. All of a sudden my hands are peeling. I had scarlet fever without knowing it. Now I just have a terrible chill but have to get up nearly every day to pick up the packages the Aryan sends me. He wants to see me no matter what and heard that I sometimes cross State Street. He arranged with Löbl when and where I go to the Viktoria with my bucket. He walked toward me on the street, and from a distance I could see how happy he was to see me. His face was beaming. We couldn't talk, of course.

He wanted to try again the next day. But I really couldn't go to the Viktoria because I didn't go to work. So I stayed at the street crossing. He crossed twice and waved to me in secret.

FEBRUARY 21, SUNDAY: I've had a sinus infection with a huge headache. I'm over it now and happily continue to peel. Every night I have a high temperature and of course have to stay home. I don't want to get chilled. I'd rather go to work. We keep talking about the bunks we're supposed to get, but we don't want them. Just when I was feeling worse than ever, I had to go to the Magdeburg and negotiate since supposedly nobody else can do it. I managed to get somebody from agriculture to look at our room. He was very kind, took an onion and garlic, and said that at the very worst we'd get bunk beds. And then I arranged with the Housing Office that if we do get the beds that Lotte and Mama will be allowed to move in with us. Then all of a sudden they came to our room on Tuesday and measured again. Our room elder ran straight to the Magdeburg, but nothing could be done. By tomorrow we'll be forced to take the three level bunk beds. We had to put every-thing in the corridor. Mommy sat on our luggage all day, and not only that, they aren't letting Mama and Lotte move in.

I made a scene at the Housing Office. They realized they were wrong, that from the very start we tried to make it clear they were caretakers and had been here six months and therefore had the right to have beds and not cots. In short, whether for this or some other reason, the next day they got a permit to move. Lotte and I live on the third level, Mommy beneath us, and Mama across the way. We have a corner just for us. We're like a family and are very satisfied. We thought the beds would be much worse. Besides, they're saying that we girls are going to be moved and soon. That would mean some advantages for us. I got a package from my Aryan with cognac, soap, tea, honey, and cigarettes. Daddy got a package from Zlin. So now we have food and then some.

MARCH 31, WEDNESDAY: I've moved again. Six of us girls from the sheep stall got a place together. It's where they housed the geese last year. Before us, it belonged to the policemen. It's a large room in the Schanzen, and they talked about giving it to us for half a year. The policemen moved out, and we were given just two days to move in. We worked for three nights until nearly morning with a couple of boys. They behaved fabulously. In three nights they built six couches, a table, two chairs, a closet, two cabinets for laundry, and a cup-board for food and dishes. Everybody who visits us is thrilled with it. This Saturday we'll have lived here fourteen days, and this is the happiest I've ever been in Theresienstadt. It's sort of like a weekend house. We always have guests. The girls are nice. We almost never fight, and we've gotten to know each other so well. We've worked together for three quarters of a year, and we know all of each other's weaknesses. Mommy and Mama visit me every day. We have a small furnace with pipes you can use for cooking, and they cook dinner every day on them. I'm happy that Mommy lives with Mama and Lotte. At least she's not alone that way. I try to devote as much time as possible to her, but unfortunately I have very little time. Egon also visits me often. Since we're the same age, he'd never demand from me what I can't give him, and it never comes up. I've explained all this to him, and we're clear about everything. Jarka hasn't visited me once since I moved into the new apartment. I don't know why. I visit Eva every other day. She still has a fever. It's about 99°F to 100°F. She isn't in pain, but I fear it's her lungs. She knows too, but doesn't show it. Fredy's almost always with her, and the girls are very good to her. At least she's not alone. Unfortunately I'm unable to devote as much time to her as I'd like.

I got a jar of cured ham from the Aryan. We also got three packages: one from the Glasers and two from strangers. We were very glad. Daddy eats dinner here with me every night. He works in the warehouse at the Hohenelber, but hasn't profited from it so far. I'm taking English lessons now and am very happy about it. A young boy comes twice a week, and we have conversations in English. Kraus, who's our boss, brought us together. He arrived from Lipa a little while ago. He's very intelligent, and I can talk to him about everything. I give him bread or cigarettes for it.

Nobody's really counting anymore on getting home soon. Everybody on the farm has moved, and we've gotten comfortably settled in. There are concerts, lectures, theater, and even a revue here every day. On the other hand, German Jews are dying of hunger in the blockhouses. What use are the thousand packages that come here daily when the same people are always getting them? Typhoid has nearly stopped. The hospitals are still full, but there aren't any new cases. If everything stays as is, we personally could survive here a very long time. Everybody says I look dazzling. I have a tan, and Mommy has put on some weight too. It's still hard work. We're shaving the sheep now. Our boss, Kraus, is anything but pleasant.

APRIL 21, WEDNESDAY: We're still living in our beautiful apartment, but we'll probably have to move this week. First of all, we'll miss the apartment because we have much more space, but we'll also miss the company. We had company every night, and when we were alone, we could read. Getting used to barracks life again will be hard. There's absolutely no reason we should have to move. The farm got an order saying we had to live together. Supposedly it came from Löwenstein. He claims people working on the farm are living too well and that nobody can control the amount of vegetables being smuggled when everybody lives scattered apart. Others say it came from Clausen, whose house was demolished in an aerial attack. And *we* have to pay for it. In any case I'll be able to devote more time to Mommy now. Even though I went to the Hamburg every free minute, I had very little free time because I had to cook for everybody. There are seven of us and with Egon sometimes eight. It's no exaggeration to say it's sometimes hard to fulfill everybody's needs. I have the constant feeling I spend too little time with Mommy. She says I shouldn't come, but I know perfectly well she'd miss me. I always try to take care of Mommy. Nothing else is as important.

Six people escaped from the ghetto last week. It will have huge repercussions for us all. Most of them were children from mixed marriages who were alone here and whose parents still lived at home. The children were homesick. Children of mixed marriages are sent here from age sixteen upward. Some of them reconsidered and came back. Since then the barracks have been shut down, but it isn't strictly enforced since it's impossible to check if everybody's going to work. The light curfew is even worse. No light is allowed in the barracks at night. Sometimes we have light, but we hide it well.

Daddy sometimes brings something to eat too, but thank God we have enough. I got some noodles and a piece of bacon from Karel again. Otherwise we receive packages from Prague, mostly from the Glasers. Aside from that I still have the potatoes. Sometimes I cook for all of us out of the things Mama and Lotte bring. We are a family and share everything. If only Richard could see us now!

MAY 5, WEDNESDAY: I've now happily moved back into the Hamburg. I live on the third floor in a large room with all the girls from the farm who had to move from outside. The order came terribly fast. Saturday both Bischitzkis were locked up because of some lost geese. Clausen, who is, by the way, drunk all the time, causes the most unbelievable mischief. People think that Poljak or one of her people did it. And now two people who've done an outstanding job creating a vegetable garden from nothing, slaved over it, are sitting in jail. That's the thanks they get. Things are extremely tense, and the farm seems to be running around without its head. Kraus has taken over meanwhile. Sunday night the order came to move immediately. Nobody expected it would happen so quickly. Easter Sunday! Beautiful Easter! We had to chop up all the furniture into pieces, and we took the wood with us. A shame we're losing the beautiful apartment. The last few days weren't all that harmonious anyway. Some things were lost, and everybody suspected each other. I don't know why, but they're all so superficial, and there were terrible things going on. I couldn't have stood it any longer. Even though none of us said anything, it couldn't be the same as it was. I got along with Eva Taussig better than with anybody, but she let herself be influenced by Hilda, who I can't stand. I never fight with anybody, but if we were alone, I'd fight with her day and night.

I'm now in a room with thirty other gardeners. They're mostly young girls, but there are also some mothers. I'm on the third level, as I was before. The only advantage is that there are five to a block, not six like everywhere else.

Both the Bischitzkis were released after a week. First Wilda, then Tonda, and now everything's back to usual. Clausen is going to leave. Supposedly somebody better is taking his place. Maybe we'll even have to move again. The only advantage to being here is that I'm close to Mommy. But it also has lots of disadvantages. I can't cook anymore, or at least very little. I can't get to any of my things. I have everything in suitcases and run up and down the steps all the time. In other words, it's awful.

I'm with Egon again quite a bit, and he's really very nice and incredibly decent. He's different from the other boys. We read together and talk. It's a real friendship. We kiss now and then. I'm happy to have somebody again.

MAY 8, SATURDAY: I'm sitting outdoors on a rock in the pasture. Leitmeritz is spread out before me. There's a divine silence everywhere except for the cuckoo calling and the birds chirping. The dirt, hunger, and hideous conditions of Theresienstadt are nowhere to be seen. It's as if it didn't exist at all.

There's freedom here, air, everything's pure, and yet it's only twenty minutes from the ghetto. I'm so thankful to be here. It's the best work you can get in Theresienstadt. Nobody in the entire ghetto has it as good as we do. We leave the city limits at 7 A.M. and return at five in the afternoon. The Eger flows by us, and we can even do our wash and let it dry in the sun.

The light curfew in the barracks is very unpleasant. We didn't notice it as much when we were living outside. Sometimes Egon leaves here at 8:30, and I'm scared he'll get into trouble on the street. It's dark at eight o'clock, and you can't do anything but go to sleep.

Karel came two times in a row. I said a few words to him through the window in the Dresden barracks. Both times he was with his wife and little son, who kept waving. He was here on Easter Monday while we were in the middle of moving, then again on the following Sunday. I got three magnificent packages again: one with a cake and candy for Mommy on Mother's Day; the second with meat, bacon, cheese, and noodles; and the third with sausage, eleven pounds of flour, a jar of fat, four pieces of fried chicken, and cheese.

I'll never forget what these two people have done for us and how wonderfully they did it. I hope I can pay them back one day.

I have an unpleasant rash all over my body. I've had it for a long time now, but it's never been this bad. I've tried everything possible, but it won't go away. I'm getting injections now. I wonder if it will help. I'm studying English twice a week again. I talk and read with Jirka Gans. He may not be a perfect Englishman, but it's enough for me, and at least I don't forget everything.

MAY 14, FRIDAY: I'm sitting in the forest, tending the sheep. They're lying down and haven't budged, so I only have to watch over them. We're enjoying nature as never before in normal life and are continually outdoors from morning to evening. The girls bring us our lunch.

Last Monday a ghetto guard came to pick us up. The six of us who were living outside had to go to headquarters right away for questioning, to Janeček. It didn't matter at all to me, though I wasn't quite convinced they'd let us go immediately. Considering the Bischitzki case, they could have also kept us there. Frau Bischitzki and Frau Klinger were still at headquarters. They were both horribly upset. I met Mama and Lotte on the way but didn't say a word about it to them. They'll find out soon enough. We were taken to headquarters and talked to the policemen. Hašek suddenly came in screaming and sent us into the same cell I had had before the interrogation that time. I was so upset and on edge that I fell fast asleep. It was a strange feeling.

We had to stand in the cell with our faces to the wall and weren't allowed to speak with each other. The whole situation seemed very funny to me. What more could possibly happen to me? For once I really am innocent and have a clean conscience as seldom before. We were taken to Janeček one by one. He interrogated us thoroughly and wanted to know what we knew about the goose story. Absolutely nothing, of course. Hašek then wrote up a report and we were released.

Egon and I are still friends. We both know it's only temporary, but our friendship is good. We get along magnificently, and if we don't see each other for a day, we miss each other. We think only about today, not tomorrow. We talk about everything, often very serious things, and we read good books together. We're not as sociable as the others, and we don't say stupid and superficial things the way the others do. I haven't been getting along with the girls at work lately.

I hardly spend any time in my room. I only go there to sleep. I'm in the pasture all day. We get money now, printed ghetto money. I get sixty crowns and Mommy, seventy. I wonder what you can buy with it. I desperately need shoes, just plain wooden shoes. I don't have any at all. I've got enough clothes but no shoes, and I almost always go barefoot. I'm really furious with Trude. I gave away about sixty-five cigarettes to get the apartment back then, without anybody knowing they were from me. Nobody else gave even the slightest bit. I gave Trude thirty-five cigarettes to take care of for the party that was supposed to happen but never did. Yesterday I asked her for the cigarettes. "The boys smoked them when they came over at night." "But that's not what they were there for, so just anybody could smoke them." I'm furious. I don't have to let myself get used that way. I want at least twenty back. None of the girls will want to give any of theirs up, and yet they all have some. I need the twenty for wooden shoes.

MAY 20, WEDNESDAY: I've been in a miserable mood lately, but it's not just another mood of mine. I'm thoroughly sick of everything. I don't know for sure if it has to do with Theresienstadt. Maybe things like this happen in normal life, just not as blatantly as here. Most of the people here say they're sick of Theresienstadt and that they want to go home. It's easy to imagine that home is like heaven, yet there are just people there too, the same as the people here. Bad people. At the moment I don't even believe any good people exist anymore. Dear God, is it possible there are so many bad people?

Is it that people are in the world just to do bad things, to cheat and exploit one another? The worst part of it is that I've adapted to it. I'm forced to. I'm disgusted by it all. How do you tell who you can trust and who you can't? Probably nobody. Are there no ideals anymore? Mommy is the only person I can always rely on. She's the only solid, firm, strong, steady, fixed point that never moves and always stays sweet. Mama and Lotte are good too. When I'm with them, everything's fine, everything's forgotten. But I'm there so little. I spend much more time with the others. At work the girls look out for themselves. Everybody tries to take advantage of everyone else, and they're happy when others have more work. I work a lot because I still enjoy my job. Then again, I get angry if I see the other girls working less.

Egon is the worst of all. Egon, who I trusted and who I believed would never be capable of doing anything bad, kept a sack of flour and claimed it was his. I still can't believe it. I have a key to their apartment because I cook there all the time, and that's when I saw the sack. I keep hoping the situation will get cleared up. Maybe he made a mistake. Everything's going as usual on the outside, but sometimes I look at him and think, Is it possible?

Vera transferred her number onto my pass. Now I have to report it missing, and there will be lots of trouble from it. The cigarettes in the shack are very unsafe. I can't take them home, and they're not safe with Egon either. Otherwise I would have given all of them to him. Everything's so terribly complicated, and I'm unhappy.

Things are getting to be too much for me. If only Richard were here. I could discuss everything with him. I'm trying to be calm and think things through, but I just can't. I can't tell Mommy everything either. It's all so terribly difficult. Eva's a problem too. Maybe it's my fault we've become such strangers. I hardly have any time for her, not even with the best intentions. I come home from work at 6:30 every day, fetch my supper, go to Mommy's, and often cook supper with the milk I bring her every day. I have a harder time making friends than the other girls. I can't find the right light tone like some of them, who can talk for hours about nothing. It all seems so flighty and uninteresting to me. Thank God, Eva's in good company. The girls take good care of her. Fredy takes care of her food, and she looks better than she has in a long while. But our friendship?

JUNE 9, WEDNESDAY: I've gotten back together with Eva through a horrible tragedy. Jarka suddenly went crazy and jumped out of a window on the second floor. He wasn't killed, but he's badly injured, and he'd probably be better off if he hadn't survived. It all happened quite suddenly. He's never done anything like it before. He supposedly inherited it from his mother. Eva visits him twice a day and reports everything to me. She hasn't spoken to him directly. He's still unconscious.

Yesterday we let the sheep pasture on a slope where there was a cherry tree with marvelous red cherries on it. Of course we ate the cherries. There were four of us. Somebody was always on the lookout. I'm standing there with a branch in my hand, and then *crack!* the whole branch breaks off into my hand. Quickly I pick the cherries. At that moment Hilda yells: "Look out! An SS man!" I threw the branch in front of the sheep, but it was too late. He came up to me and said, "What are you doing there? It's double sabotage to eat cherries and break off a branch." Then he picked up the branch and said, "Here. Take the rest of the cherries."

What a swine, I thought. He's sarcastic on top of it. But then he started a conversation. I couldn't believe my ears. "If it had been anybody else, someone from security, imagine what would have happened. You're visible from far away. Break off as many branches as you like for all I care, but don't let people see you. By the way, they're not even ripe." Hilda and Eva started to cry, they were so touched that such a thing still existed: an SS man and still human. All the upset was probably to prove to us that even among Germans there still are humans. The belief in human beings that I'd lost has returned. I brought Mommy a few pounds of the cherries. I got diarrhea and a stomachache.

JUNE 22, TUESDAY: We've been caught picking cherries several times in the meantime, but only by Jews, so we keep smuggling. The temptation is too great. Ghetto life runs its normal course, but there isn't a day when something couldn't happen. Herr SS Unter- or Oberscharführer (it doesn't matter which) Heindl definitely was sent from God to punish the evil Jews in the ghetto. He rages horribly. There isn't a day that goes by when his efficiency doesn't land someone in jail. He probably wants to make himself indispensable here so he doesn't have to go to the front. For the time being, it seems to be working. There isn't a place, a room, a hole where we're safe. He searches everywhere for cigarettes. Even the straw in the sheep stall has been searched. He must have a lot of snitches here, because he always goes for a sure thing. The security boss's deputy and the chief secretary, Klaber and Preiss, have been put in jail along with their wives. The ghetto guard has been reduced from 450 to 150 men, and they're planning to make big changes. Men will be allowed to be ghetto guards from the age of forty-five. Almost ninety percent will be new people. All men from forty-five to sixty will have to register. I wonder what will come of it.

Lots of big changes are being made on the farm. Nobody expected them. Our crew leader, Lederer, called a meeting. He wanted everything to run smoothly and brought a bunch of his people here from Lipa. He and Tonda Bischitzki had a big fight, and Tonda isn't on the farm anymore. From now on the horses will belong to the delivery service and not to the farm. Lederer's really furious about it. Horses are his passion. It's all Clausen's doing, and since he's being sent to the front, Lederer may have some success getting them back.

It's great to see that Germans con each other, too. But it's usually the Jews who end up paying for it.

The Družstvo is swarming with new people. Some of them are from Lipa along with their relatives and Protectorate children. Many of them are good at soccer, which is very important for the farm these days. There's a game every Sunday.

JULY 7, THURSDAY: I'm lying in bed with a strange illness. I've had an aversion to all food, but especially bread, for two weeks now. I feel sick if I see bread with fat on it. I had a temperature of over 100°F on Tuesday. Since then, it's been over 98.6°F all the time. I go out in spite of it but feel miserable, and often break into a terrible sweat. I wasn't planning on going to work, but the present situation is forcing me to. A whole group of people were dismissed from the farm yesterday: Karel Klinger, his mother and fiancée, the Bock brothers and their mother, and several others who've been with the farm since it began. Everybody thinks of them as being the farm's founders. They've done lots of work on it, but Herr Lederer doesn't like them. Besides, they were with Bischitzki, and that's reason enough to fire them. Erna was fired for having scarlet fever. Lederer refuses to acknowledge any illness. I'm afraid I'll be kicked out too. I don't want to give him a reason. It wouldn't be very pleasant to be put to building crates like the others who have been fired from other divisions. All the ghetto guards have been dismissed, and now they're taking only men age forty-five and up. The younger boys have been sent to hard labor, crate building, and street construction.

They've opened beautiful stores. We get money, points, a savings account, and lots of other things. How it came about is a total mystery. I'm curious to see if I can get a pair of trousers and a coat I desperately need. I had a shoemaker make some sandals for me and Mommy. Each pair costs sixteen hundred crowns. It's unbelievable! I won't believe it until I read this during normal times, and even then I won't believe it. But it's really true. I gave him two pounds of bacon for them. That's four thousand to five thousand crowns for both pairs of shoes. The bacon was from Karel, of course. So I got them free. Now I'd like to get some work boots.

Karel sends us packages tirelessly. He sent us two pounds of fat, roasted pork, pickles, and sweet rolls again. All the things he gives us are invaluable. He writes very sweet letters along with everything. Simple and yet . . . He always wants to help as long as he's able to. He says it's the least he can do for me since it was his fault I was in jail and I didn't betray him. He wouldn't be alive today if I had.

I had a real heart-to-heart talk with Eva. She's going steady with Fredy. He loves her very much, but she doesn't feel the same way about him. She needs somebody she can truly love. Egon and I are on good terms again. It's important to have someone you can talk to about your experiences. I'm learning Russian from him, and he's learning English from me. The reason I'm learning Russian is not that he's convinced me Bolshevism is the most ideal thing in the world but that I want to train my mind a bit again. I think it would be best to learn a language that's going to play an important role after the war. I don't think I can ever learn it, but if I can get to know some of the fundamentals and some words, it will certainly be of some use. I'd prefer to study English intensively, but I unfortunately don't have the opportunity. My English teacher hasn't shown up in a long while. When you think about it, it's horrible the way we're living here. It's not just the outside circumstance that we're being held captive. At the moment we're not suffering from hunger and have enough freedom of movement. What I miss most is studying. I'm probably just being presumptuous. A year ago I'd have been happy to have what I have now. But I'm always dissatisfied. If only there were somebody I could talk to, somebody who is intellectually far superior to me, somebody I could at least get a general education from. But there's no one. The girls have completely different interests. I'm reading *Madame Curie.* It's a very beautiful book. Russian is very hard to keep in my head. I can't learn the alphabet. That's supposed to be the most difficult part. Still, I want to learn so much, to have knowledge.

JULY 14, WEDNESDAY: Seidl hasn't been commander of the camp for a week now, and Burger has taken over. Since then packages have been completely suspended. Supposedly only two thousand will be allowed per month. That's fewer than we've been getting in a day. If we want to get packages, we have to fill out a form requesting that such-and-such person send a package in exchange for a ration. That's a double-edged sword. Should we give anybody's name in Prague? Their exact name and address? Won't they get in trouble for associating with Jews? Won't their house be searched? Everybody's talking about that, of course. Personally I don't believe it. That kind of rumor is nothing new. They wouldn't let us send packages from Prague because supposedly people were hanged for it here. We gave the Glasers' name. Not much could happen to them. First of all, they don't have anything, and besides, she's a German Aryan.

JULY 17, SATURDAY: I'm twenty-two years old. Yesterday I celebrated it together with Mama's birthday. I got lots of things: two pairs of men's trousers that will need altering, a jacket, two hundred crowns of ghetto money to buy myself something if possible, a laundry bag, a cake for both Mama and me, a pendant for a necklace, and a long letter from Egon. He doesn't like to write, so it must have been a real sacrifice. Fredy gave me a picture he painted himself. It's of the *parta* on the pasture. Mommy came to my bed to congratulate me early in the morning. That is, she had to climb up to the third level. Later in the morning I was congratulated by everybody in the stall. The girls gave me envelopes with identification papers and a pass. I was at the pasture from four to eight. I was given a special position with Karel. There's a very tense atmosphere there, and I'm the only one who doesn't fight with him. I'm also angry with him, but I can't be so fresh with him as the others are. We've divided the work hours from 7 to 1:30 or from 1:30 to 8. But a week ago they were changed again, and we have to work both mornings and afternoons. It's completely unnecessary, but we're being forced to weed his garden, which we shouldn't have to do. We had tickets to go swimming and wanted to go at six, but he said, "You can't go until you've finished every-thing here." Vera had a heated debate with him; in other words, they said the most insulting things to each other. She told him everything we thought about him, that he thinks he's the master and we're his slaves, that he's always walking around with his hands in his pockets watching us work. He doesn't give us any credit for our work. We're killing our-selves, and he just gives us more and more work. It doesn't matter whether we work quickly or slowly. He never lets us go home early and thinks up the most impossible tasks for us. He takes everything and doesn't give us a thing from his gar-den. Strangers come to him for vegetables, and who knows what he trades them for. While we, who water and tend them, don't get the tiniest bit. We don't get anything from the Družstvo because they think we're getting things from Kraus. "You don't know what work in Theresienstadt means," he says. "Whoever doesn't like it doesn't have to stay here." We all said we'd leave. The next day we gave notice that we wanted to be replaced. Wilda was supposed to call a meeting, but he didn't come. Karel came instead. He said that for us to change positions, we needed Lederer's consent, and that would mean being fired from the farm. This time he'll "gen-erously forgive us," on condition, of course, that anything he demands will be carried out unquestioningly, that we will obey his orders, etc. We were totally baffled. We didn't expect that. We were a little sorry to leave the sheep. We weren't doing that badly. We just wanted a different group leader. Instead of getting a better one, we made things worse for ourselves. Even though he's sweet as sugar now, we want to complain a second time. But it makes no sense. Wilda refuses to do anything, and nobody else is interested in us. "You'll have to take care of yourselves with him," he keeps saying.

■   ■   ■

JULY 22, THURSDAY: I'm with Eva every day. Today for the first time I visited Jarka in the asylum with her. She goes every day and takes him food. I admire her. I couldn't bear it. I was completely taken aback by the sight of him and the surroundings. I could never get used to it. Jarka was in terrible shape, almost unrecognizable, emaciated. The worst part was his eyes. I'll never forget them. Completely absent, and yet he would stare at you so intensely. Jarka was so happy to see me. He held both my hands tightly and laughed, and there was something so childish about him that you automatically began speaking to him like a child. The guard handles him very strangely: "Have you shaken hands yet?" "Say thank you." "Say please." "If you don't finish everything on your plate, you won't get any water." And so on. Jarka obeys him like a small child, with huge frightened eyes. You could die from the air in there because most of them are incontinent. The guards have a hideous job. I don't know how they can still be at all normal. Jarka held my hand tightly and brought me quite close. He wanted to say something. Him: "What's going on outside?" Me: "Nothing, nothing at all of interest to you." Him: "What's going on up there? Have you been up there?" Me: "No." Him: "I don't believe you. You're tricking me for sure. You're not telling me what's up there. Show me your nose." It's a strange feeling to speak to an abnormal person. You never know what they'll do next. Yet Eva tells me he's doing much better now. He'll never get out again. And we'd been such good friends.

The Grünbergers had a terrible tragedy. They were living fairly well in Slovakia for the last half year but decided to go to Hungary and were caught. Thirteen people with fake passports were taken to Pankrác prison. Danny jumped off the train, and the Gestapo searched for him for a long time. He hid in every possible place in Prague but was finally caught by the Gestapo. All thirteen people, including many Aryans and Germans, were sentenced to death by the SS. It's all so incredible. I can't imagine it, but it's true for sure. We heard about it from several sources in the last Prague transport. Can you sentence a person to death months ahead of time? It's probably a good thing Benny isn't here anymore. He'd be terribly upset about it.

It's gruesome to lock a person up and tell him he's been condemned to die in three months. Eva's upset, and I haven't even told her the worst of it. I can't tell her. She's still secretly hoping they'll come here or be sent to the fortress, which in her opinion would be bad enough. Eva thinks about Danny and Benny all the time. They are still part and parcel of the group, more than anybody else.

The last three Prague transports have arrived. Prague is now officially *judenfrei* [free of Jews] apart from a few exceptions and some mixed marriages. My cousin Doris Schwarz was part of the group. I have even less affinity with her or understanding for her here than I had in Prague. A year and three quarters in Theresienstadt can change you a lot. She's led a charmed existence up to now, lived in beautiful accommodations, eaten well, had clothes and shoes. Everything's been impeccable. She brought loads of things with her, but she has to peel potatoes here anyway.

The British and Americans have landed in Sicily and been very successful. Naturally everybody's telling each other that Sicily has surrendered. It suffices that the newspapers are writing that there's heavy fighting and that the British have an advantage over the enemy and many towns have been evacuated. There's heavy fighting in Russia too, and the British have made several attempts to land. Could the end be near? I simply can't imagine it. I'm starting to doubt for the first time that I'll ever see Richard again. And if I do, will things have remained unchanged between us? Mommy's completely certain of it, but four years is a terribly long time. He's thirty-three. How long can he wait? I'm twenty-two, and that's pretty old for a girl. What will I do? There are times when I lose my confidence and am scared I'll be alone. I've believed in the marriage for four years and can't imagine not being engaged to him.

My relationship with Egon has substantially cooled. He's a big egotist. He visits now and then for five minutes and then mostly talks to the others. He only came twice when I was sick, even though he passed by umpteen times. Everything else is much more important to him: Russian, smuggling, etc. I certainly won't run after him. I may even become a Socialist. The ground is fertile for it here. Especially when I watch how the Kraus family deals with us. You could just die seeing the way they live, not giving anybody the slightest bit of anything and thinking they're better than us. It's the class difference on a small scale here. Some people here are so arrogant, and right next to them is the most horrible misery. We're a bit better off than average. We're not hungry, but we don't have anything left over either. Lotte hasn't received any packages since the prohibition, but I've brought back twenty pounds of new potatoes, and we cook a good soup from the dog's bones twice a week. Even if we left the sheep, I'd still at least have vegetables. We'll find something somehow. Once in a while I can take fruit too, but much less than last year. Lots of things have been going on. When Kraus threw Lidka out for the second time, Wilda finally said, "This can't go on. We're going to have to replace the entire group after all." I went to see Wilda that afternoon to find out what would happen to us. We talked for a long time. I calmly told him everything that's been going on, that we didn't really intend to leave, but that the conditions under Kraus were impossible. We're treated like servants and are doing work for him that we're not required to do. We haven't received a single vegetable for it all even though the whole farm has vegetables. He decided that four of us would go to the garden and four of us would go to the Crete. None of us was actually happy about the outcome. We had hoped to get another group leader. There was a big lineup in the morning. It was just like being in the military. We weren't used to that. All the groups have to line up twice a day.

AUGUST 15, SUNDAY: I've got a day off for the first time in two weeks. Nobody had a free day during harvest. They're registering in the ghetto. Nobody knows why. Everybody thinks there's going to be more transports. A registration implies work transports. Nobody knows how or where to. If anybody at headquarters knew, we'd certainly have found out by now. Approximately five thousand people have been registered up to now. Mommy, Mama, and Lotte were among them. Daddy has been excluded for now because of his illness, but he volunteered because he has an even better reason: his gold medal for bravery. Besides, he was afraid he'd lose his position if he were considered ill. The war medal went down on his papers along with a number one. Mommy also got a number one. It supposedly means that you're working in the camp, which means here. A number two means you'll be sent away. I didn't get anything at all. Besides, they probably won't dismiss me from the farm—I'm on the protection list. Almost all the boys were released from the garden, mostly AK. I like working in the garden and don't want to go back to tending the sheep. The nicest part about being here is the camaraderie. No orders, no fighting. I don't care if there's sometimes more work. It's much better than the mood at Kraus's. It's been very hot for the last two weeks. I haven't felt it because I water the plants from 5 A.M. to 1 P.M. and have afternoons free. Besides, there's a big pool in the garden and we're allowed to go swimming there. Smuggling is a further advantage. I'm feeding the entire family, meaning seven people, just from the garden. If I were ever to tell people what we looked like every day at noon and night, they'd never believe me. My outfit consists of a large bra, sweatpants with an elastic band, and a big skirt. The others wear trousers and socks or rubber boots. We stuff everything possible into them. Right now we've got tomatoes, bell peppers, apples, pears, carrots, and cabbage. I recently discovered a potato patch, and we're smuggling from there too. The most gorgeous shapes walk by the policemen at noon and night, some angular, others round—we make quite a picture.

"Can anybody tell I've got something on me?" "Feel me. Think I can walk around like this?" "God, I'll lose a cucumber for sure in front of the policemen." "If only the *berušky* [guards] weren't there." That's of course the thing we fear the most. Hiding things is of no use at all. They bring Aryan women from Leitmeritz once a month, and each time several people fall victim to the policemen. Usually they're people from the field who don't know better. One of the girls always walks ahead. If everything's okay, she comes back and yells something to us. If they're there, she doesn't come back. The policemen aren't allowed to touch us. We can't be too obvious, of course. He could ask to have a woman inspector sent. Some of the girls are so experienced, they take fifteen cucumbers at a go and nobody sees anything. But that's just for sport. All I care about is taking care of our daily needs. I trade cucumbers for bread. You can get anything for vegetables. I bought two pairs of shoes.

I've also received things from Karel again: seven pounds of sugar, five pounds of flour, two pounds of fat, twelve apples, a box of *šumáky* [flavored tablets] for lemonade, a chicken, a squab, an apple strudel, and a lot of plums in one week. But that's over now. Löbl told me it's very dangerous, and he won't let Karel risk it anymore. He has three children, God forbid he should get into trouble. He was a bit hurt in his last letter that my parents have never written him. Of course, I wrote him a long letter immediately. I explained that Daddy was ill; Mommy added a line or two as well. It's hard to believe that there are people in the world who live just to help others. Sometimes I wonder if Richard still thinks about me or if he hasn't long since married. Maybe I'll have a big disappointment in store. Have I waited all this time for nothing? Has he found another wife in the meantime? Sometimes I feel really miserable and get an inferiority complex. Will I be too old to find somebody when the war is over? Egon's definitely not for me. I'd prefer to call it quits with him. I think he'd like that too. I'm getting along with Eva very well again. Fredy adores her.

The fleas and bugs are a horrible bother. All Theresienstadt is so full of them, it's impossible to exterminate them. Everything had to be moved out of the Sudeten barracks within forty-eight hours. Maybe we can move back in again, but I don't want to move in with the same girls as before.

AUGUST 18, WEDNESDAY: Starting today, they've forbidden us to wear coats outside city limits. We're going to freeze for sure when it gets cold or rains. There are very strict inspections going on everywhere. Otto Bock was put in jail because he had something on him. Tomorrow they're going to fumigate. They always do nine rooms at once. Little by little the entire Hamburg barracks is being deloused. Even though we've had fewer bugs in our rooms than in the others, the whole barracks was filled through and through with them. I'll sleep at Mommy's for two nights and Eva's for one. Transports have been canceled again. Nobody's being registered anymore either. There's a sad reason for it, though: we have dysentery here, infantile paralysis, and cerebrospinal meningitis. There are over three hundred cases of dysentery. Exactly the same as last year. Frau Goldschmied has it too, and she's feeling very bad. She's a fabulous person and self-sacrificing, which is a very rare thing in Theresienstadt. She's taken such good care of the children and now needs to be cared for herself.

I'm still seeing Egon now and then. We've become totally indifferent toward each other. I'd like to meet a new crowd. I bought myself a pair of shoes for two thousand crowns. I have to be careful with smuggling now. Pepík Reiner is starting to notice me. It's cruel of him because I don't take any more than the others, and besides, I certainly have more reason to do it than a certain Frau Freiburger, who has gained thirty pounds here and got a beautiful apartment and extra rations from the council elder. I have seven people who depend on me.

AUGUST 22, SUNDAY: Yesterday there were big inspections going on as we went in and out. The *berušky* searched us thoroughly, mostly for ghetto money. It didn't bother me in the least. This morning a transport left from the small fortress. It contained almost all women. Nobody knows where it's going, probably to a concentration camp. They each carried a small bundle with them and looked very bad. I stared my eyes out but couldn't recognize anybody. Seventeen people left the ghetto this afternoon and went to the small fortress. Mimi Kominik and her sister were among them. There were many others who I only know by name. I can't understand it. A person like Mimi who's always beaming, cheerful, and brave, being sent to the fortress for a letter she wrote about eight months ago when she'd go to the pasture with us. Poor Mimi.

There was a huge celebration in the Magdeburg barracks this evening. I went. Egon invited a girl I didn't know. It was the best opportunity to end our relationship. We're going to stay good friends. He needs somebody else, because I'm taken. I slept in Mommy's spot on Thursday, in Dr. Morgenstern's on Friday, and at Eva's on Saturday. We slept on the roof on planks and mattresses. It was a good group. Richard surely wouldn't blame me if I were to go out with somebody here. Does he even think about me anymore? If I had just one word from him, it would calm me down; then nobody could blame me. All I want is a word, and I'd happily put up with anything. I'd be satisfied. Anything but the awful uncertainty of not knowing where you stand. Eva's going steady with Fredy, and it's very intense now. Their relationship has changed. Eva really loves him.

AUGUST 29, SUNDAY: It was an unpleasant week. I felt horribly alone for the first time. I was miserable on Sunday. I'd just returned from Eva's. All the girls there had boyfriends. It's completely normal for them to be involved in a relationship, but I felt very abandoned. All of a sudden Egon came to see me on Monday night, and I was really happy to see him. He said he'd been looking everywhere for me.

There was a huge scandal in the cow stable on Thursday. Somebody discovered milk was stolen. The entire stable crew was instantly replaced because of it, Egon included, of course. He's very unhappy and doesn't know what he'll do. He told me he's got a girlfriend, but they don't know what to talk to each other about. She's apparently very dull. Since then he's visited me every night. We're talking again like we used to.

The transport specter is back. Everybody's afraid, terribly afraid. It doesn't seem to be a work transport. It'll probably end up being an ordinary Poland transport. They've remade the list three times. Some people knew exactly who was in it. Everybody packed. For now all the Weisungen who have been in jail since June, that is, since Burger's been in command, are supposed to go. Another 150 former ghetto guards and all the AK had to register. And anyone elegantly dressed was immediately sent by Burger to register. Mostly big fish. It didn't matter if they suffered at first or not. People who came in work clothes were sent away. The registration seems to be something of a Weisung. Even the AK isn't protected anymore. Everybody's scared. We don't know if we're in the transport or not. We have nobody who can check. I don't think my parents are in it because of Daddy's gold medal. Besides, Mommy's a nurse, and they're supposedly protected. If I'm put into the transport, then it could only be a Weisung, but it's a year since I was in jail. Mama and Lotte are very afraid, but I don't think they have reason to be. Mama's too old for a work transport, and besides, she's a nurse, and Lotte has children under fourteen.

The wildest rumors are circulating again. People seem like little children, believing everything they hear. One moment they're rejoicing, the next they're in despair. Everybody's all upset because of the transports. "It'll never end," they say. But then transports are postponed for a couple of days, and everybody's happy again. "We'll be going home in two months, and things are fine." You have to take everything with a grain of salt. I can't understand how people can be like that. A former field group, the four of us from the sheep stable; Margit who tended the pigs; and fifteen boys are working in the garden now. The *parta* leader is extremely disagreeable. We completely ignore her. She constantly claims that her group doesn't smuggle. She actually does smuggle very little and works like mad, but you certainly can't say that about her group. That can only mean we're the ones doing all the smuggling. If I do take something, it's only because I badly need it; I dislike doing it intensely. If you're tempted to do something you don't want to do, you shouldn't do it, because something will go wrong. Lately I've taken very little, sometimes nothing at all. I get so nervous that I tremble when I pass a policeman. Those few minutes twice a day test my nerves horribly. It's hard to take for any length of time. And now is the best time to be smuggling—there are so many vegetables. But I have to force myself. We're badly in need of any vegetables we can get, especially now. Lotte has stopped receiving packages. For some reason neither our nor their ration coupons for packages have arrived in Prague. Lots of people still get packages, up to forty-five pounds. Each person is allowed one a month. Lotte's friend Gustav wrote that her ration coupons hadn't arrived, so he couldn't send anything. We depend on what I can take from the garden. It's been going well so far, and the children even had some fruit and vegetables. We trade vegetables for bread. Potatoes are more difficult. I have to scratch them out of the ground with my fingers and hide them in my pants, but that doesn't work well. Karel came today after three weeks without a word. I saw him once at the Dresden and on the way back from the garden, but I couldn't speak to him. It's probably better that way. We could easily land in the fortress if somebody saw us.

■   ■   ■

There's a ghetto law here, but whoever doesn't fall under it, for example, people with Aryan contacts, goes to the fortress. I admire Löbl's ability to withstand the nervous tension and can completely understand him when he complains how much he'd like to quit. The nights must be horrible. I got another package from Karel on Sunday night: two pounds of fat, two pounds of honey, a bar of soap, two cucumbers, and a loaf of bread. A loaf of bread costs four hundred crowns, a cigarette, forty. The prices are totally outlandish, and it's getting to the point where we don't know what to make of it anymore. That's the difference between people who have everything and people who have nothing at all. There are people here who earn unbelievably large amounts of money and those who have to sell their last piece of clothing dirt cheap; for example, a magnificent winter coat that cost twelve hundred crowns, or a tomato that cost fifty crowns.

Twelve hundred children came here on Wednesday from the Ukraine. They were between the ages of two and twelve and escorted by SS. They were in terrible condition, full of lice, filthy, and in rags. They were deloused for a whole day and night. They are all without parents. Their parents were killed about two weeks ago in the most gruesome way. Speaking to them is forbidden under penalty of death. The doctors and nurses who have been appointed to take care of them had to take their baggage and break off all communication with the camp. Before long we found everything out anyway. The children had seen their parents being chased into gas chambers. Some of them were killed in pogroms.

There have been twelve cases of infantile paralysis. Keeping it isolated here is very difficult.

■   ■   ■

Transport fever. This time it stops for nobody, whether old or young, whether longtime resident or not. Families are being torn apart. Five thousand people from the Protectorate have been sent away. Yesterday afternoon twenty-five hundred more people were chosen for the transport, at 10 P.M. the next night twenty-five hundred, and this morning the reserve. So far, no one in our family is in it. I don't want to breathe a sigh of relief yet. Anything is still possible. Everybody who doesn't happen to be in this transport has relatives or friends who are. Almost everybody I've spoken to so far is in it, including many from the farm like Tonda and Wilda, who've helped keep us here. What will the farm be like without them? I can't imagine the farm without Wilda. Fredy Hirsch was thrown in jail for talking to the Russian children, and now he's going. Frey, the leader of the ghetto guards, and 150 former ghetto guards are going too. Dr. Janowitz, Löwenstein supposedly, and many others are going too. I'm awfully afraid for Mama and Lotte. I hope they won't be in it. The transport was awful. When you met somebody on the street, you wondered, "You're still here?" "And you too?" Last night everybody went to the gathering areas. Everything was processed at the various yards in the Hamburg, Kavalier, Genie, Bakery, etc. The first yard in the Hamburg was barricaded for the transport, and you could only talk to people from a distance. Each person was only allowed to take what they could carry. People sat on their luggage all night. It gets pretty cold by morning. People were taken to the station at intervals throughout the day. None of them had slept the last two nights. Indescribable scenes took place in the Magdeburg. People argued over who had better nerves and who could endure it the longest. Wherever Zucker walked or stood, there was a line of six or seven people behind him, all of them talking at him simultaneously and shouting over each other. He'd throw them out one door, and they'd come back in the other one. And yet it's so easy to get somebody out of the transport. You simply take a card out of the transport file and stick it back into the regular file. Naturally somebody from the reserve list needs to take their place. There were a lot of volunteers, mostly children registering to be with their parents. The worst thing is seeing families being torn apart. There are almost no families that haven't left someone here, and then the person left behind thinks maybe they should have volunteered after all.

Everybody from the farm who didn't volunteer has been pulled out. Lederer reconsidered at the last moment, and Tonda and Wilda are out too. Thank God!

Yesterday afternoon and today we were confined to the barracks, but nobody paid any attention to it. Anybody could leave if they wanted to. On the other hand, anybody caught outside by Heindl would be put in the transport. People are going crazy from this eternal toing and froing.

The transport is gone, and life goes on. There were horrible scenes at the last moment. People on the train were still being pulled out of the transport while others were being put in. Utter chaos. Then came the calm after the storm. For two days it was all people could talk about, and suddenly even that stopped too. Supposedly it was the last one. But as of yesterday they've started talking about another one. Now all of us are certain to be going. None of us can have any illusions anymore. How come only people from the Protectorate keep going? The Germans are desperately unhappy here. The old people are completely alone, starving, yet the ones who've grown somewhat used to things here are being forced to leave. The misery of the old Germans is beyond description. They walk from room to room all day, begging for a piece of bread. Others sell their last shoes, clothes, underwear. I bought work boots for a tomato one day. I also gave the man a cabbage, and he was thrilled. Normally I only take as much as I need for us and perhaps something for bread too.

There isn't much left to take in the garden, and things are getting more difficult. There are five people watching us all the time. On Wednesday, Kraus, not our previous boss, told me to come and see him. He was with Grass at the Leitmeritz meadow and had spoken to Karel. It's terrible: Karel speaks to total strangers and asks them if they know me. He just happened to ask a friend of mine who just happens to be a decent person. But he didn't have to be. Karel left a message, saying he wanted to talk to me. I wrote a few words back. Then Kraus came on Friday and brought me a beautiful wristwatch and a letter that nearly made us both cry. Karel wanted me to take the watch as a souvenir so I would never forget him. If things went really badly, then I was to sell it for bread. But he hoped I'd never find myself in such a situation, and if I did, he would do everything in his power to prevent it. If I'm ever put into a transport, he wants me to tell Löbl immediately so Löbl can report it to him immediately. He doesn't want our family to go, no matter what. I'm not supposed to tell anybody, but he's got a way of keeping us out of the transport, and he'll use every means to make sure we stay. I wrote him a long letter and sent it to him through Kraus. Now I was in a quandary. Should I tell Löbl? He'd be very angry about Karel talking to strangers again. But I have to tell him anyway. So I went to see him. He was amazed and then of course angry. Half an hour later I heard about a terrible catastrophe. Approximately twenty people were arrested and instantly taken to the fortress for associating with Aryans at Leitmeritz. Oh, God! It must have been

Karel. I raced from the garden straight to Kraus. He was at work. It must have been he who was seen giving the letter to my Karel. I imagined the whole thing in gruesome detail. It would be easy enough for them to get my name. And then Löbl and the rest of the group would all land in the fortress. I raced to Porges, where Kraus works. They wouldn't let me in without a pass. Luckily I ran into Kutscher, who told me the whole story in detail. There are men who are leveling the land behind Leitmeritz. Heindl had them searched and found a lot of things on them. So, it wasn't Karel!

I don't know how I made it back. My feet were like lead. The fear went straight to my legs. This time things ended up okay. But for how long? Even though I have nothing to do with them directly, I'm in as much danger as the others. Mostly I fear for him, a father of three small children who has done incredibly good deeds. I want him to live to see the end.

Italy has surrendered. The Germans are condemning it as the betrayal of the century. The next day Rome was occupied. Naturally the wildest rumors are circulating again, and the mood in the ghetto is as if we were going home by next week. But the transports damper the mood a bit.

OCTOBER 8, FRIDAY: A year ago today I was thrown into jail. That was a horrible day. I'm so tired all the time, I can't get any reading or writing done. We haven't had a day off in two weeks. We've been working in the fields mostly, and Lederer's really pushing us.

OCTOBER 10, SUNDAY: People complain about the work, but I'm just glad I have it. It's the only thing that halfway makes sense. Today I have a day off and am much more aware of how awful this life is. I'm alone most of the time now. I miss having a group of friends to visit in my free time.

I've begun to doubt lately whether I'll ever get together with Richard again and that everything will be the same as it was before. I simply can't picture it anymore. Since I've lost this firm belief, since I no longer have any idea of my life, future, hopes, and plans, I'm very unhappy and wonder what the point of it all is. Does anything make any sense anymore? It's certainly not Richard's fault. I used to be proud of having saved myself for him for so long or having fought against everything. Now I'm not proud anymore. Now I'm just sad, and it's impossible to make up for it. It's time to stop whining now. Nobody can see on the outside what I'm really feeling. I'm cheerful, lively, and don't show my true feelings at any cost.

A year ago I was doing much worse. Yesterday was the Day of Atonement. Many people fasted. The farm had to work, of course. It's unbelievable how most of the old people who are starving and normally go begging from room to room for a little soup fasted just the same. How strong their belief must be.

OCTOBER 17, SUNDAY: The turnip harvest was very bad. It was cold and dirty, and there was a mad rush. We had to harvest in the fog early in the morning. At noon it got a bit warmer, but at night it was so cold, we could barely move our fingers. My hand was full of blisters. Lederer walked back and forth constantly, yelling, "Work! Work! Faster! I won't let you go home until everything's done and it's nighttime." Then there was the celery harvest for two days. Again it was terribly cold. Smuggling was very unpleasant because it was so dirty. Some girls were so stuffed, they could barely move. They're insane to smuggle so much. They'll get us all in trouble. But there are always people who know no moderation. Frau Morgan, for instance, the wife of our previous headmaster. Once she smuggled two hundred tomatoes into the ghetto—and from an Aryan field to boot.

The last few days we harvested tomatoes. First, though, we had to harvest all the turnips and celery, and in the meantime all the tomatoes froze. That's probably the German system. About a wagonload of tomatoes had to be thrown away. They were hard as rocks in the morning. Later they thawed and turned to mush. Thirty thousand vines filled with tomatoes. That's no small matter. We worked in the afternoon from one to seven and came home in the dark. Nobody had anything against us smuggling anymore. I had 150 tomatoes. Frau Morgan had 360. I'll never forget the walk home in the dark past the policemen. One of the workers had a real hump on her back from all the tomatoes. We went harvesting a few more times for spinach and one day in the garden for leeks. They are the most sought-after vegetable.

We have more than enough in terms of provisions. We made puree from the tomatoes, and bought stockings and scarves with them besides. The whole ghetto is going to get some. That's a sign of how much there is. I got a package from the Glasers two weeks ago. It didn't have many valuable things, but we could use them all, especially for cooking. It was obviously scraped together from several families. The Kohns and everybody contributed something. Lotte got two packages from the Sudeten. I got two sausages, ten cheeses, two jars of fat, and two of meat from Karel.

Italy has declared war on Germany. It's being fought on Italian soil. The Germans have retreated from Russia and are on Polish soil. People are expecting another front at Calais in the next few days. Many claim the British have already occupied it, but that's probably not true. There's just an offensive there, probably to prepare for an invasion or force Germany out of Russia. Still, I don't believe in a speedy end to things.

The children from the Ukraine were suddenly packed up with all their caretakers and sent away by train. Nobody knows where they're going. Supposedly to Sweden or maybe Switzerland. The caretakers will probably accompany them to the border and then be deported to Poland. Two transports have come from Denmark, one with local emigrants, mostly young boys and girls who were living on estates there to be retrained and then leave for Palestine. They didn't get there, but they were doing fabulously in Denmark. We got very bad reports from Birkenau about the last transport that left from here.

OCTOBER 24, SUNDAY: It was a terrible day a year ago.

Smuggling is risky again, though at times it's pretty calm. The nights are dark, so I was able to get another package from Karel: two sausages, two pounds of margarine, and two pounds of fat. We often have horse meat, minced meat, or meat with barley to eat. That's a big improvement. Besides, we cook an abundant dinner every night from the vegetables, and I've put some weight back on. I visit Jarka every other night. He's always terribly happy when I come. He's still lying in the Hohenelber with both legs in casts. He's completely back to normal. He and Eva are my only friends. Every Wednesday there are lectures on agriculture, agricultural machines, botany, and soil cultivation. It's very interesting to hear something theoretical after learning through practice.

■   ■   ■

OCTOBER 31, SUNDAY: Wilda and Tonda were taken to the small fortress yesterday. They had been at headquarters for two weeks, supposedly for something they did a year ago, letters or something of the sort. The entire farm is furious. Many more friends have been sent to the fortress: Frieda Dubsky; Pekárek, who left a small child behind; Renée Jelínek, the most influential woman in Theresienstadt. She knew all the policemen and Germans. A painter, a boy who married a girl in Eva's room four months ago, and many more were sent, altogether twenty-six.

I'm still receiving packages from Karel all the time. Since Saturday, I got about forty pounds of flour, four pounds of fat, margarine, butter, cake, two jars of honey, ten pounds of apples, ten pounds of onions, fourteen pounds of sugar, four pounds of smoked meat, and other things. You can't compare that with the normal packages. I feel very uncomfortable about getting so much. It's more than I need and puts me to shame. Every day at noon Ada Löbl sticks his head in and I know I have something to go and pick up. He's very careful and doesn't want to do anything to attract attention. Everybody teases me about him. Karel's preparing for winter, and I'm convinced we'll be able to get through it comfortably with all these things. But it's too much all of a sudden. I don't know where to put it all, and I'm terrified of inspections. I write to him every day that it's too much and I don't want any more.

NOVEMBER 7, SUNDAY: I've received twenty more pounds of apples from Karel and nothing since. Mama got a forty-four-pound package. Thank God it's got no food. But it's been terribly uncomfortable for her to be constantly taking food from me. She's quite unhappy since Karel's been sending us so much. She's very nervous and fights with Lotte sometimes. I've never fought with her or Mommy. She's angry that Gustav visits all the time and doesn't bring anything. The children are often a nuisance. They scream if they don't get everything immediately because they know it will get them something. They should be brought up better, but that's very difficult here. They know that I always have apples and that they can always get them. But I don't want to give them everything at once, or we'd run out right away. Lotte got a small package from Lisbon, six pounds of figs. It probably was sent by Bedřich from Chile. Finally some news. Otherwise we don't have the slightest contact with foreign countries. It's inconceivable that we haven't received any answer to the two cards we sent to Switzerland. What's going on with Richard? Why does he remain silent? Lots of people have received news from England via Switzerland; only we haven't received a single word.

Theresienstadt is full of good news again. Roosevelt is on his way to Teheran. There's a huge conference in Moscow, a peace conference supposedly. It's the first time an American president has journeyed to a conference. There must be something big going on. I'm sure it isn't just negotiations. We're hearing new reports that there will be an end to the war and that we'll be going home this year. But that would take a miracle, and I don't believe in miracles. Despite all the good news, the mood is very tense. People are arguing everywhere: in the washroom, in the food line, in the shops. They make *šmeliny* [black-market deals] everywhere. Nepotism is the rule. You can't get anything without greasing somebody's palm or through friends. At first it really upset me, now I do it too and can't imagine it otherwise. I have more than most people. When I see how people fight over two pounds of flour or three pounds of sugar, I realize what treasures I have. And vegetables to boot. I bought warm shoes, the sweatpants I've wanted a long time now, slippers, lace-up shoes, socks, stockings, everything I need. The ghetto's overflowing with clothes, probably even more than are available outside. It's the German Jews who've brought in the most magnificent things, and they sell them all for food. Prices are constantly rising. Bread costs six hundred crowns; a cigarette, fifty; sugar, one thousand; an apple, one hundred; flour, twelve hundred, and vegetables have an enormous value. Everything's used for trade: bath tickets, laundry, laundry permits, theater tickets. Theresienstadt has a high cultural standard. There are daily concerts, lectures, opera, comedy, etc. I regularly go to them. There's some sort of lecture every night, mostly for young people, sometimes about politics, sometimes about art. I usually go with the girls. I spend very little time with boys. I'm also taking frequent English lessons and have supposedly made progress. There's a lecture every Wednesday at the farm. I visit Jarka all the time, and that always cheers him up. I seldom see Eva. She's with Fredy all the time, and I'm in the way. He sleeps with them now and is usually there during the day as well.

We're freezing pitifully at work. It's below freezing every morning. We dig and the ground is frozen. Sometimes we go into an unheated room to warm ourselves against each other. Smuggling is hard too. You're half frozen and you're supposed to put ice-cold cabbage or icy spinach next to your body and then the ice starts to thaw. But we need to take this last opportunity as long as there's still something to take. At least we come home to a heated room. Other girls who live in the attic are even colder at home. We heat every day even though heating is strictly forbidden. We always bring planks or wood back with us.

■　　　■　　　■

I'm lying down after my typhoid injection, but I have to be at the Dresden by two. Karel's coming.

NOVEMBER 11, THURSDAY: It's five in the morning. We were awakened at twelve midnight. Everybody had to line up at 5 to be taken to Bohušovice. Supposedly to be registered. We were told to dress warmly and take some food. What's that supposed to mean? The general opinion is that we're going to be sent away. Our room was very upset, and we disturbed people still sleeping in other rooms. Everybody packed, everybody vacated the premises, everybody got dressed over and over again. Personally, I don't believe they'll send us away. Then again, they did serve us an order to provide lodging for some sick old men who'll probably steal everything from us, but that doesn't matter at the moment. It's indescribable how things look. Everybody's racing around, doing things that make no sense. I'm completely calm, and so is Mommy. If they want to shoot us or send us to Poland, we can't do anything about it anyway, though maybe we'll even survive that.

NOVEMBER 14, SUNDAY: We got back home at 10 P.M. after a horrible day. At seven in the morning, we were taken to the Bohušovice basin by barracks and blocks and stood there, some until nine, others until twelve. The worst part was that we didn't know until the last moment whether we'd be going home or what they meant to do with us. It was just an ordinary census, only the Germans wanted to turn it into a campaign to worry and harass us. It was horribly cold, even though we dressed in layers of our warmest, most essential things. I also had the most indispensable food and cleaning items with me. The mood never turned bad all day. We saw it was only a census and we'd be coming home in the evening.

So we are back home again. We stood in rows of five hundred. The Jews counted us about fifty times. The Germans counted us twice. Men and women were separate. No sooner did the Germans turn their backs than everybody rushed off and searched for their families. I was very close to Mama and Mommy. An order came every five minutes: "Back to your places immediately!" and everybody ran and stumbled over one another to their places. That's how it went the entire day. The children were amazingly well behaved. You seldom heard a child crying. The old people were worse. They fainted or got cramps and had fits. We were pretty tired and finally just lay down on the bare ground close together to warm ourselves. The lavatory situation was terrible. Either people went where they stood, or they spread a blanket around themselves, or they went into the trough under the posts where the policemen were guarding us. I'll never forget how when evening fell, everybody started running toward the ghetto at the same time. It started to rain. Our room held together tightly as though our luck depended on us staying together. Everybody said they'd never let us go back home, so there was no point to it. But everybody still ran in the same direction, simply because nobody wanted to stay behind. Of course we couldn't get too far because it got congested. We'd go two steps and stand for half an hour. That lasted until nine in the evening, and we still didn't know if we'd be let back into the ghetto. Children were crying because they'd lost their mothers. Old people were falling like flies because after standing for fourteen hours, they couldn't take it any longer. Some of them lay down overnight in the barracks closest to where they were standing. Our room gradually lost one another too, and I was left together with Lidka as my bed neighbor. We held each other's hands tightly and wouldn't let go at any cost. We finally elbowed our way out of the crowd to where lots of policemen were standing. From there we ran as fast as we could to the ghetto. What a feeling! The ailing old men from our room were gone. We were never so happy to be "home" as we were in that first moment, because we truly doubted we'd ever be coming back. We quickly cooked something warm, and beat our mattresses, and jumped into bed. We slept like corpses.

DECEMBER 10, FRIDAY: We've been counted three more times in the meantime. Edelstein and Faltis, the director of the records, were jailed for allegedly swindling people during the transports. In short, the census isn't correct. Everybody removed from the last transport had to line up within two hours. They were then sent to the fortress as they were, and some were fresh out of bed.

Everybody had to be in bed every night to be counted. Then there was another census, which went alphabetically. There were Germans sitting in four places with a line in front of each of them. You had to wait for hours to hand over your identification papers. Some stood for eight hours. We were there for only three. Even here there was nepotism. If you had a friend, you didn't have to wait at all.

A Swedish commission was expected at the beginning of the month. Lots of preparations were made. They removed the third level of the beds everywhere, and the people who had to move were placed in the barracks where first the Ukraine children and later the Germans lived. It was almost like a transport. Whoever had connections could stay; the others had to leave. Some were on cots, others on the ground. The rooms are definitely more comfortable now. I have a good spot by the window and a wall for me and Lidka. Sweeping and washing the floor are better now too. We have a *polička* [shelf] on the wall for clothes, and there's even a wardrobe too. The same thing happened a week later to Mommy. It was much more upsetting there. Lotte was really afraid she'd have to move. But everything turned out fine. Lotte was extraordinarily happy and ordered a cabinet immediately. Then not a week later, before the cabinet was even ready, the giant, fearsome transport specter appeared again and destroyed everything. Everything, everything was different, every joy spoiled. The most horrible thing has happened: Lotte and her children are in the transport.

DECEMBER 20, MONDAY: I have to start much earlier if I really want to write everything down that happened. I hope I won't forget anything. We were celebrating the feast of St. Nicholas. Everybody in our room gave everyone else a little something, and it was nice and cheerful beyond my expectations.

The following Sunday, I visited Eva and there was dancing. I went to a lecture almost every night. Most of them were very interesting. Karel sent us things in short intervals, so we had more than enough food. Lotte was worried about Jana because they supposedly found something on her lung after her flu. Our relationship with both of them, and especially with Mama, has been especially warm lately. We made plans for Christmas, thought about presents for the children, what we'd give each other, and everything ended up so differently.

On Friday the tenth, Fixler came and told Hilde and me to go to the corn harvest. The two of us worked with six boys. Altmann, the supervisor, is a German with a big swastika, but he spoke good Czech and was quite easygoing. He kept going away, so we could smuggle more easily. During the ten days we were there, two transports left. The first was for Wednesday the fifteenth, and Lotte and the children were in it. She'd known about it since Sunday, of course. But absolutely nothing could be done about it. A group of friends tried to get her out. She was in the reserve but had to line up in any case and got another number in the sluice. She was unbelievably calm, packed continuously for two nights, and never believed she'd get out. Mama was in a terrible dilemma over whether to go with her. Everybody strongly advised against it, and after a long while, she decided not to. Eva's uncle came on Monday and told me Eva was in the transport. I ran there immediately. I hadn't even considered the possibility it might happen. Fredy has volunteered to go with her. I helped her pack. She had very few things. I brought her food. The only relief is that Fredy's going. That way the poor, sick creature—because she is very sick even though she looks good—isn't totally alone and abandoned. She's quite calm. She's only worried for Fredy and is packing mostly for him. How can I help? I might not be able to be one hundred percent true to the promise I made to her parents. But I know that Fredy loves her, adores her, and that he'll take care of her as nobody else could.

Tuesday morning before work I took her some fat, canned food, sugar, and apples. I had to go to my damn job, and here I had such important things to do. I managed to speak to her again before noon. Fredy hadn't been summoned yet and was very nervous about whether they'd take him. People are begging and praying in the Magdeburg, and they don't want to take them. We took Lotte to the sluice with Steiner in the afternoon. She had lots of luggage, and we had to take a cart. Mama said good-bye to Lotte and the children, and then I went home with Mama. How many such farewells will we have to go through? How many times without knowing when or even whether we'll see each other again? That's the worst thing about Theresienstadt. Lotte held up fabulously. I brought her dinner and some things she'd forgotten. It was a huge struggle to get inside at night. There were various sluices going on. The Jäger barracks were cleared, and all the boys were housed in the attic in the Hamburg. They kept coming to us half frozen to warm up. The entire ground floor of the Hannover is a sluice, and so are all the manufacturing barracks. Eva was in the Hannover, and it was impossible to get to her.

The numbers for the whole transport were changed during the night, and it was done alphabetically. The whole street was lined up for the transport when I came home from work. It was very cold. Burger behaved terribly. He acted like a beast, slapping people who got in his way, pushing people into carts with or without their luggage. He didn't care. In the end he needed more people for the transport, so he just took anyone walking on the wrong side of the street with no luggage, and those who had luggage had their backpacks torn off them because there wasn't enough room. Twenty-five hundred people left, and the next twenty-five hundred were called for Thursday the sixteenth. There was a huge racket in the Magdeburg. Burger had lists brought of all the administration, production workers, mobilization of labor, provisions, etc.; in short, of everybody who had been most protected. He chose people completely arbitrarily, names he didn't like, and they were simply Weisungen.

Egon came to me at 7 A.M. His mother's in the transport. He's volunteered and asked me to help him pack. Of course I helped him all morning. Then I went home to check if we weren't in it too. Mama's in the reserve! We didn't expect that. Mama had finally calmed down in the last few days and was even glad she'd decided to stay here with us. She couldn't have helped Lotte anyway. Lotte is energetic and brave enough. But she certainly would have volunteered to be with us if we had to go. And now she's in the transport! So once again we packed. Steiner is sweet and good. He helped Mama a lot. She's high on the reserve list. I was with her in the sluice all afternoon on Friday and Saturday morning and afternoon.

We waited for the train. It came late in the afternoon. The moment of truth. Names had been called out since 3 A.M. for those with normal transport numbers. I stayed with her the whole day. Mama isn't in it. By six o'clock it was ninety-nine percent sure she'd be staying. I went to get her some dinner and meant to pick her up from the sluice at seven. Then I heard that the entire reserve had to line up. Some said it was just to survey them, others said there were five hundred people missing. It was a horrible mess. Women began to wail.

I stood there as if hit by lightning. I looked and looked and couldn't find Mama. Did she have everything with her? Her sleeping bag? Is there anybody able to help her? I ran to the Jäger barracks. There sat Burger at the table with an overhead lamp and two coal ovens at either side. He had an entire staff of people waiting for a sign from the lord and master. Poor Mama! It was dark farther back. The bushes were crawling with people hiding to escape their fate. People in the Jäger barracks hid under beds, behind beds, under planks, on the toilet. There were entire families hiding, and if they were called, they simply didn't come. It seemed to work. Mama didn't hide for sure. Mama would go immediately if they called her just once. If only I could find her. If only I could see her and help her. She's so alone. Heini Brock won't be able to take care of her. He doesn't know her number. Wilda Heller won't be able to take care of her either in this terrible mess. If only I could get a pair of overalls like the transport helpers! I spoke to several of them, begged them to let me borrow one. No, they couldn't, and if people were missing or something wasn't in order, then the entire transport administration and the helpers would be put into the transport just as they were. That's what happened to Otto Kraus.

It was simply impossible to find Mama, and so I went home heavyhearted, trembling with anxiety. If only I could have seen Mama one more time and said good-bye. I've never been so helpless. So far I've managed to get into every transport assembly I wanted to. And now this one that's so terribly important is gone, and I didn't find Mama. We're so powerless. I couldn't sleep all night. I went to the sluice at five in the morning, thinking she might still be there. A tiny ray of hope. I found a group of friends there who'd somehow managed to cheat their way out of it. A few of them said she might still be there. I went to the office. Lots of numbers close to hers are there. Hers is crossed out.

I was terribly unhappy for the next few days. The whole world is gray on gray again. I didn't speak to anybody. We have to move. They're turning our room into an outpatient section. We have to move now, but we'll have to move again in a week anyway. We've got an unbelievable number of things. Mostly food. I don't think anybody has as much as we do. Approximately twenty pounds of fat and all kinds of things in large quantities. What can we do with it? We can't possibly eat it all.

Christmas Eve was very sad. I went to see Jarka and took him some food. Then I went to my parents. Mommy was sweet. She'd prepared a lot of little things for me. I'm awfully grateful to her. She senses how unhappy I am about being alone, and it wouldn't have been so bad if Mama, Lotte, and the children were here. Now it was just the three of us. I cried for the first time in a long while. New Year's was the same. We wanted to invite some of the boys from the farm, but we heard there would be a spot check, so we postponed it until Saturday afternoon. About twenty people came. We ate, played the harmonica, and sang. If only I weren't so alone. I went for a walk with the boys on Sunday. Then we wanted to hear the requiem, but we weren't allowed in.

There was a to-do in the Jäger barracks. Heindl and Burger and some SS burst in and arrested a lot of the boys. A few of them were playing cards for large sums, others were smoking, etc. Somebody must have reported them. People were being arrested all night. They were probably betrayed by the first group once they'd been beaten. Nobody has a clear conscience. I was afraid for the Löbls, but they weren't there.

We're working in the garden again. We have an ideal workday: eight to ten and one to three. One day during the corn harvest, Lederer came by and screamed, "What are the women doing here? Women have no business here. You've lied to me, all of you. You've done it behind my back!" Altmann did everything he could to keep us there. He listed all the advantages, but Lederer wouldn't be reasoned with. I met Löbl three days after what happened in the Jäger barracks. He looked terrible. Me: "What's the matter?" Him: "My brother's arrested." So the arrests have continued. Besides that, they went to get somebody from the attic and did an inspection while they were there. They found a lot of cigarettes, money, and masses of food with the Löbls. Löbl's brother was instantly thrown into jail. The next day they got the other brother, who was in the Hohenelber hospital. I visited Frau Löbl twice to find out what was going on. I didn't dare go to see Ada, but he wasn't home anyway. Just before that I got a lot of food from Karel.

1944

JANUARY 1, SATURDAY: Margit Forscher, Martha Holz-bauer, Elly, Magda, and I have been working in the greenhouse for the last few days. It's a privilege for us, and we're very happy about it. I waited for Karel in the Dresden on Sunday, but he didn't show up. Sunday evening Frau Weisel said, quite by coincidence: "Do you know who they've put into jail, Evička? I'm sure you remember the railway man responsible for getting you into jail last year. Well, he was arrested for bringing a suit-case into the ghetto. It probably has to do with the Löbl busi-ness." All I said was: "Hmmm. I vaguely remember him." I felt as though I'd been given a blow. I wasn't able to say another word. It can't be. A person like Karel, who's risked his life for us daily. He's had such an incredible guardian angel that we truly thought nothing could ever happen to him. He's been too good for something to happen to him. Besides, I'll be drawn into it too. I had to take Mommy some things even though I'd rather not have: fat, preserve jars with meat, anything that stands out. It didn't matter whether they had my name yet. I'd be involved anyway. It's fairly certain they'd get it. For one thing, I was sure there was a letter and package for me in the suitcase, and then they would do a house inspection and most likely find letters from me there. I had an unpleasant night. I slept no more than an hour altogether and had terrible dreams. I'd wake up with a start every time there was a noise and think, "Burger's coming to get me." I prepared everything just in case they did come and I had to leave immediately. I prepared my alibi, but nobody came. I walked around in this state for two days. Tuesday afternoon there were two men standing outside the greenhouse after I finished work One was Jirka Neumann, the other a man from Löbl's group. Jirka: "Karel sends his greetings and some cookies." Me: "What's happening with Karel?" Him: "Nothing, everything's okay." Me: "You mean he's not in jail?" Him: "No, just the opposite." Only later did I understand what he meant by his answer. I was beside myself with joy.

JANUARY 12, WEDNESDAY: I went to a lecture at the Družstvo in the evening. Suddenly Zwi called me outside and told me my mother supposedly wasn't well. The man who had brought the message from Karel was standing outside and said, "You have to come with me quickly. Karel's here and wants to talk to you." I had no time to get upset. We walked across a pitch-black yard and over planks to Sokol Hall. Now and then a flashlight shined on us. We came to a shack. It was completely dark, but you could feel people's presence inside: a few cigarettes lit up, muffled discussions. There were four or five men in there. I couldn't tell exactly. Somebody came up to me from the corner. A flashlight lit my face for a moment. It was Karel. He took both my hands and said, "Good evening." He shook my hands affectionately. The men went outside after a few moments, and I was alone with Karel. We sat on planks, and he began to talk. He spoke in short, broken sentences and told me everything that had been weighing on his heart since we last spoke. That was the day I was put into jail. He told me how worried he had been about me, how he'd tried to get in touch with me, how he would drive around Theresienstadt every day just to see me, what he gave people just to get a word from me, and how often it was all for nothing.

The men came to pick me up at eight. Karel quickly gave me a bunch of apples and a newspaper, and we left. I was completely dazed. It all seemed like a dream. But it was real. I ran to Mommy's and told her everything.

JANUARY 13, THURSDAY: A lot of people have arrived from Germany, people who up to now were considered Aryans. They were in mixed marriages and had Aryan children, but now, according to the law, are suddenly considered Jews. Four women came to our room. We thought they were snitches; at least, that's the impression they gave. It was unpleasant having them in the room. The entire Löbl family has been thrown in jail. Mother and sister too. They were badly beaten by Burger and Heindl but didn't betray a thing. There was a rumor that a barracks for people of mixed marriages would be made available. Some said it would be the Dresden, others the Hamburg, and we calmly lay down to sleep. Suddenly in the middle of the night we were ordered to evacuate the bottom level by morning, without removing a single piece of wood. That'll be the day! It was particularly hard because of Mommy. Mommy has such an awful lot of things. I can't describe them all. She also has the things Mama and Lotte couldn't take with them plus everything she's accumulated in the one and a half years she's lived in the room.

JANUARY 14, FRIDAY: There has been a huge chaos since the early morning: carts driving, suitcases being lugged. We slept quietly and then began packing. We had until eleven to evacuate, but that was impossible since we didn't know where we were going. Supposedly the farm was going to take care of us. Fixler promised to arrange things, but all we knew was that we'd probably get one or two rooms in the West barracks and they weren't evacuated yet. Mommy had to stay in the attic of the Genie barracks for the time being. How we were to get her luggage up there was a mystery to me. All the corridors were filled to the brim with people lugging suitcases. Everybody was hurrying, scurrying, and upset; men, women, and children alike. It looked like a frightened anthill. Mommy finally got packed. It was almost impossible to count her pieces of luggage. I fetched a wheelbarrow from the garden. I met Arthur, a confidant of Karel's, on the way. He told me Karel was coming that night and I had to go see him. I took the three heaviest suitcases of food to Daddy in the wheelbarrow. It was a terrible job. A couple of the boys came with an oxcart to pick up our things and take them to the Družstvo. We were ordered to move to the West barracks, but there was no room for us there. We went back to Fixler in the Družstvo. He couldn't help. He went to the Magdeburg again, but got no answer. Mommy and I took everything piece by piece up to the attic. It was horribly cold. We had to stuff up a hole directly under the roof. Now we could see how hard things are when you're alone. Daddy couldn't help. Everybody else had men to help them. The two of us had to do everything all alone. I had enough friends, but I told them, "Don't bother. I can manage on my own."

The decision to send us to the West barracks came that afternoon. It was an area previously reserved for suitcases. The beds are about three inches above the ground. Margit saved a place for me in a room with some Germans. The spaces looked like doghouses. You could only crawl inside, and there was absolutely no space for luggage because the beds were too low to put much under them. I loaded some of Mommy's heaviest things, things you couldn't lug up to the attic, into a cart, and shoved them under my bed. Then we had only a little more than a foot of space left.

■   ■   ■

We left the mattresses in the Družstvo and were able to get some planks of wood from the barracks. I ate dinner with Mommy in the attic and then went back to Sokol Hall to see Karel. It was exactly like last time. Karel's like a little child sometimes. I couldn't imagine that he was the person who'd risked his life for us and could be as hard as steel, who'd gladly crawl for many yards on all fours for us. He gave me apples and a newspaper again. I ran and got to Mommy at eight. She wouldn't have slept all night otherwise. They didn't want to let me into the barracks, but I managed anyway. "Just a kiss. I'm alive. Everything's fine." Then I went back home. I was dead tired with all the excitement. What a day!

JANUARY 15, SATURDAY: The living conditions are terrible. You can't move in or outside the bed at all. Mommy's situation is even worse. It's so cold in the attic, she comes to me to get warm. The only ray of light is that I'm with Margit. I was in the shack behind Sokol Hall again at night. It's such a strange feeling. It's like being in another world. I lead a different life during the day and night. It's a double life. It's like a conspiracy in the night. The boys make a room from some planks. A light from a flashlight shines one instant and goes out the next. Karel always talks a lot. He told me he likes me very much. I believe him. He's proved it to me so often for the year and a half since we met. He never asks for anything in return, and there's never the least prospect of it either. What he's done for us is simply unbelievable.

JANUARY 16, SUNDAY: It's strange. All of a sudden I've become attractive to boys again. There's been a change in me. I talk to all the boys. I've lost that awkward feeling I had whenever I talked to someone or was with people. Everybody has somebody except for me. That's over now. After all this time my confidence is back, and all at once I have lots of admirers. Every day I go out with someone new and we talk. One of them lives in a tower, a fantastic apartment, but otherwise he's a big schmuck. Well, for talks he'll do. Jarka's cousin Fritzek Braun is a little too short for me. T., who after being just friends for so long, has suddenly discovered he has feelings for me and is being quite persistent. Otto Kellner is completely different from the rest. He's quiet, doesn't show off, doesn't have a beautiful apartment, isn't persistent or annoying, and isn't a schmuck, and I like him the most by far. I have no idea if he feels anything for me. He's never shown or said anything of the kind, but I like him. I wish I knew more about him and could talk to him.

Every Sunday afternoon we spend time with the boys who work the land. They used to come to see us in the Hamburg, and now we go to see them. It's evening. Everything's back to normal again. I even go to Sokol Hall alone now. Jirka Neumann isn't too pleased with the whole situation. He barely looks at me. Well, what can I do? Karel is hardheaded. Once he's got something in his head, he won't let go. On the other hand, he's as naive as a child and easily swayed and wants to give me everything I could possibly wish for. He's definitely not a bragger, but he must be very well off.

They fumigated the Hamburg as soon as we moved out and reopened it three days later, but nobody was allowed in without a pass. Mommy, who's an employee there, may be allowed to move in again. There's probably a transport coming. Nobody knows anything definite yet. People seem to think there will be a quarantine for a while, and we're afraid it will be like the time the nurses had to travel with the Ukraine children when they left. Mommy couldn't have possibly stayed in the attic any longer. Apart from the filth, the air was so cold at night, she couldn't get any sleep at all. At last she got to move back into

Wichtige Mitteilung!

Schlafgelegenheiten

Für die Unterbringung bis zur Abfahrt muß jeder Transportteilnehmer Matratzen oder einen Strohsack selbst beteilstellen.

Diese Schlafgelegenheiten werden vom Sammeldienst gleichzeitig mit dem Gepäck aus der Wohnung abgeholt.

Es ist demzufolge unbedingt notwendig, die Strohsäcke, bezw. Matratzen, mit den betreffenden Transportnummern auf beiden Liegeflächen so zu versehen, daß auf diesen beiden Seiten weiße Leinenflecke aufzunähen sind, auf denen die Nummer deutlich sichtbar geschrieben wird. Gouche-Matratzen dürfen nicht mitgenommen werden.

Feuergefährliche Gegenstände

Wir machen nochmals ausdrücklich darauf aufmerksam, daß es strengstens verboten ist, sowohl im Hand- als auch im Mitgepäck

Rauchwaren, Streichhölzer oder Feuerzeuge

mitzunehmen.

Was ist auf den Vorladungsort mitzubringen

Die in den Erklärungen zur amtlichen Vorladung unter diesem Titel angeführten Gegenstände a) – h), insbesondere Dokumente und Wertpapiere, müssen ins **Handgepäck, nicht ins Mitgepäck** verpackt werden.

JÜDISCHE KULTUSGEMEINDE

A 4/566 · MAT · Jd. X. 43 · 13 m · A. D.

Důležité upozornění!

Spací podložky

Pro ubytování až do odjezdu musí si každý účastník transportu připraviti buď žíněnku nebo slamník.

Tyto spací podložky budou odvezeny sběrnou službou z bytu současně se zavazadly.

Je tudíž bezpodmínečně nutno, aby slamníky resp. žíněnky byly opatřeny po obou stranách příslušným transportním číslem a to tak, že budou přišity na obou stranách kousky bílého plátna, na které je nutno zřetelně napsati příslušné číslo.

Kaučové žíněnky nesmí býti vzaty s sebou.

Předměty nebezpečné pro vznik ohně

Znovu důrazně upozorňujeme na to, že je co nejpřísněji zakázáno bráti s sebou jak do ručního, tak do velkého zavazadla

kuřivo, zápalky nebo zapalovače.

Co musíte přinésti na místo předvolání s sebou

Předměty, uvedené pod tímto titulem ve vysvětlivkách k úřednímu předvolání a) – h), zvláště pak doklady a cenné papíry, musí býti zabaleny **do příručního a nikoli do velkého zavazadla.**

ŽIDOVSKÁ NÁBOŽENSKÁ OBEC

Doplnění a změna vysvětlivek k úřednímu předvolání

1. Označení zavazadel:

Do každého zavazadla musí být nahoře vložen lístek, který má obsahovat kromě transportního čísla jméno, příjmení a datum narození účastníka transportu. Pište zřetelně!

Tím se mění bod 3 c vysvětlivek.

2. Pro majitele domů:

Referát pro přenesení domů na Auswanderungsfond má novou adresu a nové číslo telefonu:

Praha I, Norimberská třída 32, telefon 626-22.

Tím se mění bod 3 f vysvětlivek.

3. Lístky na potraviny a mýdlo, kmenové listy na uhlí.

Mimo lístky na potraviny a na mýdlo musí každý účastník transportu přinésti:

a) kmenový list na potraviny, pokud na tomto kmenovém listu není zaznamenán nikdo jiný než účastník transportu sám; jinak je nutno odevzdat místo kmenového listu na potraviny řádně vyplněný připojený formulář „Přihláška kmenových listů";

b) kmenovou přihlášku pro odběr topiva (lístek na uhlí), pokud účastník transportu odebírá na tento lístek na uhlí topivo pouze pro svoji vlastní osobu. Jinak je nutno uvést na „přihlášce kmenových listů" shora uvedené, číslo kmenové přihlášky majitele bytu;

c) v každém případě připojený formulář magistrátu hlavního města Prahy, řádně vyplněný a potvrzený všemi dodavateli potravin.

Upozorňujeme výslovně na to, že účastníci transportu, kteří spotřebovali více lístků než odpovídá době až do nastoupení na místě, kam jsou předvoláni, musí očekávat nejen potrestání, ale i to, že na místě příjezdu bude jejich zásobování přiměřeně zkráceno. Stejně ohrozí své řádné zásobování všichni, kdož nedostojí přesně předpisům uvedeným pod 3 a — c.

Židovská náboženská obec v Praze.

ABOVE: This is the document that arrived at Eva's house telling her family they had to leave. It also told them what they could bring, where to go, and where they would stay until they were deported to camps.

RIGHT: An amendment to the letter detailing additional items to bring like soap, toiletries, etc.

INSET: The original yellow star Eva was forced to wear with the German word for "Jew."

ABOVE: The cover of one of the
notebooks that makes up the diary.
The Czech reads: "Whatever is
written shall not be forgotten."

RIGHT: The diary was written in
German shorthand.

OPPOSITE: A drawing of Antonia
Mändl done by a patient in
Theresienstadt.

THERESIENSTADT
1944

H. COHEN.

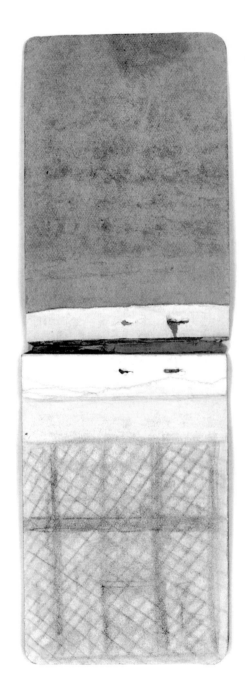

RIGHT: A faded pencil drawing done in Eva's notebook by Fredy Kantor. It shows Eva behind bars and was meant to cheer her up.

ABOVE: A drawing made in the camp by Fredy Kantor of the illegal swimming hole where Eva and her friends were photographed. The drawing is titled: "It was and will be again."

COPIES.

RELIEF COMMITTEE OF JEWS FROM CZECHOSLOVAKIA,
128 Westbourne Terrace,
London, W. 2.
                    Date 23.10.44

Dear Sir:

We are glad to inform you that we have news from a neutral
country that:

              MAENDL, EVA, Westgasse 16/4 in Terezin

has sent a personally signed receipt of a food parcel, sent
to her through the Czecho Relief Action. This receipt
dated from the month of..............

The receipts have so far not arrived in London. We shall
inform you immediately after their arrival You will then
be able to verify the signature. Owing to the great number
of equal or similar names the possibility of error cannot be
excluded.

_____

Dear Sir.   Date: London, 10.11.44.

        By the present we are glad to inform you that we have

now news from a neutral country that:

              Mr Ernst Maendl   in Terezin
              Langestr. 11
has sent a personally signed receipt of a food parcel sent
to him through the Parcel Relief Action.

This receipt dated from the month of APRIL/MAY 1944.

                    Relief Committee of Jews in CzechoSlovakia

        (Both signatures were in same hand-writing)

ABOVE: A letter from the London-
based Relief Committee of Jews
from Czechoslovakia stating that
Eva received a food parcel.

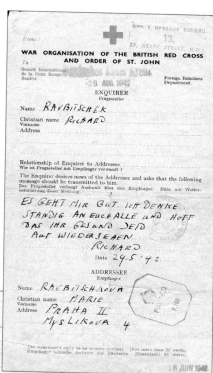

**WAR ORGANISATION OF THE BRITISH RED CROSS
AND ORDER OF ST. JOHN**

From:

WMO X MESSAGE BUREAU.
13.
27, HEATH STREET, N.W.

To:

Comité International
de la Croix Rouge
Genève

Foreign Relations
Department.

29 AUG 1942

ENQUIRER
Fragesteller

Name *RAVBITSCHEK*

Christian name *RICHARD*
Vorname

Address

Relationship of Enquirer to Addressee
Wie ist Fragesteller mit Empfänger verwandt?

The Enquirer desires news of the Addressee and asks that the following
message should be transmitted to him.
Der Fragesteller verlangt Auskunft über den Empfänger. Bitte um Weiter-
beförderung dieser Meldung.

*ES GEHT MIR GUT. ICH DENKE
STANDIG AN EUCH ALLE UND HOFF
DAS IHR GESUND SEID.
AUF WIEDERSEHEN.
RICHARD*

Date *29.5.42.*

ADDRESSEE
Empfänger

Name *RAVBITSCHKOVA*

Christian name *MARIE*
Vorname

Address *PRAHA II
MYSLIKOVA 4*

The Addressee's reply to be written overleaf. [Not more than 25 words]
Empfänger schreibe Antwort auf Rückseite. [Höchstzahl 25 worte]

1 6 JUIN 1942

---

*HOCHERFREUT ÜBER DEIN WOHLBE-
FINDEN. LOTTE, KINDER, ICH GESUND.
ANNIS AUFENTHALT UNBEKANNT.
VON EVI, IHREN ELTERN, BEIDEN
GROSSMÜTTERN OHNE NACHRICHT.
ZWEI NACHRICHTEN VON BEDŘICH.
KÜSSE MUTTER.*

26. VIII. 1942.

2 2 SEPT 1942

ABOVE: A letter from Richard
delivered by the Red Cross to
"Mama," his mother, which reads:
"I am well, I think about all of you
constantly and hope you are well."

LEFT: His mother's reply on the
back: "I'm delighted you're well.
Lotte, the children, and I are
healthy. Annie's whereabouts are
unknown. No news from Evi, her
parents, or both grandmothers.
Heard twice from Bedřich. Kisses,
Mother."

OPPOSITE: Karel Kosvanec, the
Gentile railroad worker who
smuggled food and supplies to Eva
in the camp.

the barracks. They seem to have made a mistake since all the nurses from the Hamburg automatically got to stay. Mommy had to run all over the place but finally got a pass and moved back in. That afternoon we dragged everything back with much effort. Every custodial man and every ghetto guard made things hard for us. Mommy would hand me her pass through the window to get me inside. She has a nice place. It's just uncertain whether she can stay. The room is still quite empty. The two of us cleaned up and put everything in place. Mommy slept there even though it was strictly forbidden.

It was terribly chaotic when the transport came the next day. Several streets around the Hamburg were closed off. It was all so confusing. The barracks had to be evacuated immediately, and Mommy is without shelter again. This eternal uncertainty and constant toing and froing is horrible. Mommy is on duty at Sokol Hall. She is working in the encephalitis unit. Every night she signs up for voluntary service because she has nowhere to go. Encephalitis is a new disease. Supposedly it occurs only rarely in normal life. It's actually a brain disease and usually has serious repercussions. So far there have only been light cases of it here. People sleep a lot and have high temperatures, headaches, and dizziness. There are other signs as well. You can see it in the eyes. The scary part is how quickly the disease has spread. There are lots of cases, particularly in the youth homes. There are whole rooms of it. It's very contagious, only nobody knows how it spreads. The disease itself isn't serious. The relapses are worse. It can come back two or three times.

We're planting lettuce and radishes in the garden. It's nice work, but the weather's very cold. Our group is going to be switched: Crete for the garden. The Hedi group is going to the Crete, no exceptions, and the Crete group is coming to the garden. It's very easy there. It'll be less easy in the garden, where part of the Hanka group is going. In fact, some of the members of our old group will be staying. The four of us who take care of the sheep will stay with Margit. That's good. The next day that was changed again. Lederer will allow only twenty-five girls in the garden, so now some have to leave. Probably Elli and Hilde.

I see Karel almost every night. He always brings so many things and asks me constantly what else I'd like. But I don't want anything and have more than I can use. I don't get home before ten at night. I'm "helping Mommy in Sokol Hall." Doctor Fantl always sees me home because of the ghetto guard. I'm leading a very exciting life, but I couldn't endure it for long. I'm terribly nervous. I've never been this nervous in all my life. Tears come to my eyes whenever anybody says anything to me. Usually for no reason. It's probably because of the constant stress I'm under. During the day I can talk to people better than in a long while, probably to let off steam from the night before. I laugh and have fun going out with three boys at the same time. I hope I can manage to keep them at a distance. I've wished for so long to have a group of friends, and now I have more than I want. After much toing and froing, we were given a section of another room. We moved in with a bunch of Germans, but that doesn't matter. We're just happy at least a few of us are together.

We moved on the first of February. I'm living on the third level with Eva Taussig. Margit's under me with Eva's mother. Altogether there are thirteen of us from the farm. Otto helped me to move. He took all the luggage from the Družstvo, made me a *polička*, etc. I finally have all my things and can get organized. That was impossible in the old room. T. helped me to carry some things from Mommy in the afternoon. Mommy likes him. I less so. I went one last time to Sokol Hall at night. We've stopped for two weeks because the moon's out. I went home at eleven. I told Eva a love story. She has no idea. Only Margit knows. She understands. She's often been in a similar situation.

In the meantime Mommy has moved back into the Hamburg. She found all her things in order and kept her spot. The mysterious transport turned out to be a perfectly normal transport from Holland. It contained an awful lot of luggage. People were told they should bring everything they owned: money, jewelry, smoking paraphernalia, and then everything was taken away from them. Mommy's working as a ward nurse in the sickroom. She has lots of elderly Dutch people and has a bit more work than before. Otherwise everything is the same. She's able to cook for me and Daddy again, and we meet at her place for dinner every night. Sometimes Daddy brings food. He gets things from various kitchens, and Mommy warms them for him at lunch. He's happy again and in a good mood. But then one day a note came from public health saying he wasn't allowed to work anymore because of his tuberculosis. He was terribly upset and wrote a petition right away. We don't know anything yet. He's still working for the time being. It would be terrible for him not to work anymore.

It was like spring all January. There were a few days below freezing and no snow at all. Then a frost came in February, and it snowed every day. The garden's full of sprouts, and they'll freeze over. Now we've gotten an order not to heat anymore. There's no coal in the ghetto. Up to now we've been using the heating. The wooden rooms heat more easily, and it was often nice and warm, especially on the third level. Now we're freezing. We can't even warm up our food with the little wood we're able to smuggle. The potatoes are another catastrophe. Since early February there have been no potatoes in Theresienstadt. For dinner we get a few peels floating in the so-called potato soup. Otherwise there's barley three times a week that nobody can bear to look at anymore. I still think it tastes pretty good. The rest of the days we get *buchty* [buns], dumplings with sugar or with goulash. Now and then we have a porridge made from barley, margarine, and sugar. It's awful.

The boys are starting to get on my nerves. I finally got rid of the "Schmuck." Fritzek Braun is nice, but I really don't know what for. T. isn't so easily dissuaded and often waits outside my room for two hours. When I tell him I have no time, he just comes back the next day. Anybody else in his position would have given up long ago. I'd rather go out with Otto than anybody, but he's so shy. Sometimes he's even unfriendly and very proud. We went to a concert together, without tickets of course, and while everybody stood outside waiting at the front door, we sneaked into the back office and heard everything perfectly. We held hands, and it did me good. Is it very bad of me to like somebody? With Mama gone, my last connection to Richard is gone. I don't even know if he's alive. We've taken a walk together every night since that evening. We talk about all sorts of things, mostly our previous life, and we get along well. Sometimes he can be very funny and playful. He's only quiet and serious when people are around. Our daily walk has become a habit, and I'd miss it a lot. It's very cold out, but we don't feel it. We have heated debates, and they warm us up. He knows everything about me by now; I know less about him. I don't ask. He tells me bits and pieces about his life. He's had a hard life. His father died when he was sixteen. Even though he was the youngest, he had to take over the farm because his two older brothers had professions. He went to school besides, so it wasn't easy. Then they had to escape and lost everything. He worked as a coachman on other people's property. As a Jew, he wasn't allowed to take an administrative position, but everybody liked him a lot. Then he did construction and plumbing work, and then the transports began. He went to Krämer and got a good position there. The Germans kept him for as long as they could. Then he came to Theresienstadt in the CK transport. He'd been engaged to Ditta Mautner in Prague and came here exactly a year after her, but they discovered they didn't belong together anymore. That was a huge blow for Otto, and it's only through me that he's recovered from it. He turned into a lone wolf. We never talk about the future. It's as though we don't want to destroy something. He isn't healthy. He has a stomach ulcer and is sometimes in a lot of pain. It's terrible to see him in pain and trying to cover it so I don't see. But I do and can't help him at all.

He knows just about everything about Karel and isn't happy about it. But that's my business, and he can't convince me otherwise.

Friday the eighteenth came. There was no moon, and Arthur came to get me. The shack wasn't there anymore, and we met in the laboratory. Karel had been to our house in Prague. He took them my letter, and because Frau Kohn complained about having very little food, he took her a lot of groceries right away: about twenty pounds of flour, fat, and lots more. It was difficult, but he took it back to Prague the very same night. All because she's our friend and has been so good to us. That's how Karel is.

I've got plenty of food again, chocolate too. We met two more times in Sokol Hall and took a walk from there through Theresienstadt. Karel wanted to see everything. The three of us walked together, me, Karel, and Arthur. Karel was in the middle, and Arthur was really afraid we'd run into someone we knew. We walked to the Hamburg. He wanted to meet Mommy. He spoke to her. He does everything he puts his mind to.

Lederer has to leave. Kurzawe is our only boss now. Burger is gone too, and Rahm has taken his place. The ghetto breathed a sigh of relief. Rahm is somewhat better. He can slap people around too, but a beast like Burger is hard to find, and nothing worse could come in his place.

The entire Löbl family was released. Thank God! I was really happy. I'm not going to be able to meet Karel anymore. I even prefer it that way. At least so I thought, but I didn't count on Karel's stubbornness. He wants to go on behind the Löbls' backs with just Arthur. That's really unpleasant for me. It's terribly difficult to say no. He's done so much for me. He and Arthur came to get me at eight o'clock. Arthur was terribly nervous and was afraid that we'd meet one of the Löbls. We took an hour's walk again.

The next day Löbl apparently found out I'd seen Karel. It would have been impossible for him to have found out from me, though Arthur assumes he did. Ada Löbl came to see me the next day. We had a long talk. He did find out and insists that we stop. He wants me to write Karel a letter. This betrayal thing is nonsense. It may have even been Arthur who betrayed us, and now they want to tell Karel he found out from me. Karel might finally agree to stop meeting me if they told him I can't be trusted. That's always the only thing Karel has ever asked of me in return for everything he's done. Silence is my only thanks. How will he take it? I promised Löbl not to meet him anymore. The letter has to be cleverly written. I'm not aware of any guilt on my part, but I can appreciate Löbl's fear.

It's just no business for women. I'm afraid to get my parents or Karel into trouble. That would be the most horrible thing.

Arthur came again the next night. He wants me to come with him. Karel insists on having a talk with me. But then he didn't come because Löbl put the entire Sokol Hall under surveillance, and that made it impossible for Karel to get inside. Arthur came again the next night, and I had to go with him. We ran a real obstacle course, squeezing between fences, ducking under planks, bumping into boards, listening every moment for moving objects. Arthur ahead, I behind, some of the time on all fours, always careful not to make noise because a policeman could be standing fifty yards ahead of us. Finally we came to a barbed wire fence. Behind it a tree moved, and then suddenly the signal came from Karel.

He came closer, and so did I. We could only speak at the hedge. We sat in the snow because it was more comfortable. I told him not to be angry, but we couldn't meet anymore. He understands. I was there for about half an hour. Karel is convinced I didn't betray him, and that's the main thing. He believes me, understands everything completely, and agrees. Then we went back along the same obstacle course.

Otto was really worried, and I was happy I had it all behind me. I was able to reassure him too. It was completely quiet for two weeks.

I've become more and more friendly with Otto in the meantime. He's not without his faults; he can be moody, reserved, easily offended, and stubborn, and sometimes I can't figure him out. But I like him a lot anyway.

■   ■   ■

I got a card from Switzerland. Grete Duchesne wrote that she got my card and forwarded it to Richard. He'll certainly be happy about it. I'm insanely happy. She wrote a very sweet letter. She told me how glad she was to hear from me and that I'm working on the farm. What's most important is that I may finally have made a connection to Richard now. If I'd known that Otto would get so serious about us, I might not have started going out with him. I took the whole thing very lightly from the very start. I didn't want anything serious, just some fun. But he takes it very seriously.

MARCH: There are still no potatoes in the ghetto, only dumplings with sauce or meat or barley. It's unbelievable how much flour they use on us. It's astounding. Sometimes we even have marmalade. With the half-portion supplement at lunch, you can get pretty full. After much toing and froing the girls in the farm were also allotted the supplement. We've got coal again as well, so if we smuggle a lot, we can start heating again every day. It's ridiculously cold now. There's no spring at all. There isn't a day it doesn't snow. Sometimes we wake up and there's a thick layer of snow outdoors. And it's March.

Rahm's made an excellent start. He's ordered flowers for all the hospitals. He wants everybody to be employed in their previous professions as far as possible. It's rumored that cigarettes won't be contraband anymore.

We don't have to salute uniforms anymore, neither policemen nor the SS. That's strange. A transport of two hundred young boys left the ghetto to build barracks in Germany. Our manufacturing barracks are being torn down and sent to Germany. Supposedly they're for the innumerable homeless Germans who lost everything during the aerial attacks. We hear the sirens almost daily here as well. At night and often around noon. We can be quite calm here in the ghetto. In fact, we're very happy about it. But in Germany it's their greatest fear. We can't imagine what an aerial attack means. Usually thousands of people are killed and double that lose all their belongings. Finally there's war in the heart of Germany, right where it's most unpleasant for them. The Russians have crossed the Polish border. They're waiting at Odessa in the south. Tarnopol's in Russian hands.

I found out much later that Arthur left with the transport of two hundred workers. It's strange he didn't say anything about it, especially since I'd spoken to him that very day. Maybe things were getting too hot for him because of Karel. I'm almost glad Karel has no way to meet me anymore. I hope that horribly unappealing boy in the group isn't going to take over now. I believe him capable of all sorts of bad things. I don't like the fact that he knows about Karel, but he was very good friends with Arthur. I'd really like to warn Karel about him. I wouldn't want to put myself into the hands of such . . . Besides, he certainly wouldn't keep his mouth shut.

Nine people have been "de-ghettoed." They all had valid Hungarian or Swiss passports and had supposedly been invited by their relatives. They had to pack within half a day and be on standby at headquarters. Some didn't want to go because they didn't want to leave somebody behind. A well-known family was overjoyed. The first transport home from here! Their stars were removed in front of headquarters.

I don't go to lectures anymore. I'm sorry about it, but I just can't get to them. It's Otto's fault, but it's the same for him, and we made a resolution that when we got to know each other well enough, we'd study together, go to lectures, educate ourselves. Sometimes we do go to concerts. Besides that, I spend a lot of time with Jarka. He's doing quite well. He's been out now and has even visited me twice. He suddenly hemorrhaged one night and had to be taken to the Genie barracks. He has tuberculosis and had to go back to bed. God knows for how long. I go to see him frequently. He's very sad, even though he doesn't completely understand it all. It's no sacrifice for me to take care of him and carry him food. It isn't idiotic heroics either. Everybody advises me not to go because of the danger of infection, but I have this need to help, and I help wherever I can. There's so little anybody can do anyway. At first Otto was angry that I was devoting more time to Jarka than he thought necessary. Now he understands. Pepík Reiner, the boss of all the gardens, also has tuberculosis and won't be allowed to work anymore. It's alarming how the disease is spreading.

Work is unpleasant now. In February and March there was terrible weather, and we had to work from seven to eleven and from one to five. We're planting lettuce, kohlrabi, and cabbage, plowing the soil, and making manure piles. It's terribly hard work, and we're always wet. We stand there soaked all day in the snow. If only it would decide to be spring!

Every woman in the ghetto has to sign a paper saying that she'll report any pregnancy immediately.

Sokol Hall had to be evacuated immediately. It has a movie theater, a dance hall, and a respectable prayer room. Furthermore, there's obligatory schooling for all children from six to fourteen years of age. That's the best thing they could have done. It has great meaning for all Jews. We'd become a nation of criminals if our youth were brought up with no schooling and grew up learning only how to smuggle. Things may start improving, because up to now, it has been strictly forbidden to teach the children, a rule that most unfortunately has been adhered to.

We're suddenly allowed to give birth again, and abortions are now punishable.

Ring Square is being spruced up with fountains, a music pavillion, and a park. What it's supposed to mean is a mystery, but I'm sure there's some reason for it. Probably somebody's going to visit from a foreign country. That they'd go to all this trouble out of love for the Jews is an unlikely assumption.

Karel is often here again, and I get packages of food and newspapers through Löbl. We don't meet anymore. Löbl wields a great deal of power over him.

APRIL 1, SATURDAY: It's finally spring. Everything's green in the garden. The first radishes have been delivered and smuggled. I got a package from Lisbon. It could only be from Richard. Strange, just as I was about to stop believing he still exists, he makes his presence felt. All these years I had no news from him, but I firmly believed in him anyway, and now I finally have news. It's a difficult problem, but I don't want to think about it now. There's no point to it.

APRIL 10, MONDAY: The Russians are advancing rapidly. They've captured Kovel. There's fighting in the streets in Odessa. Will there be an end after all?

I go to the citadel with Otto every morning from six to seven. We're studying world literature. These are wonderful hours, and even though I'm missing sleep, I wouldn't give it up at any price. It's high season in the gardens. We've been working through Sunday for three weeks now. Sometimes having no time for yourself can drive you crazy. There's already a lot of lettuce, and everybody's busy smuggling. I haven't been in any condition to smuggle these days. I find it downright disgusting, and the only way I have things is if others give them to me. Who should I smuggle for anyway? I'm not dependent on it. It's not worth putting myself in danger. I'm with Otto every night until nine. We both long for an apartment where we can be alone and not always in the street or in a room with twenty strangers.

MAY 1, MONDAY: Yesterday Otto and I had a day off, and we were alone together for the first time in an attic. It was a big decision for me, and I was really afraid.

A meeting was called at lunch, and within a few hours a transport of around forty men was summoned. Ten of them were from the farm, lots of good friends. There were not good reports from the previous one. A lot of them were sent to a concentration camp for associating with Aryans. Arthur was among them. He did such big things here, and then he gets caught for something petty. An adventurer, but a good fellow.

The Germans are awaiting the offensive daily. The Russians are advancing; Birkenau apparently is being evacuated.

MAY 25, THURSDAY: My neighbor Eva is sick. Everything possible seemed to be ailing her. They finally pinpointed the problem: a liver infection. She got worse and worse every day. Two weeks later she went to a gynecologist. She's pregnant. At first only Jirka and I knew. Should she tell her mother? I went to the Hohenelber right away and negotiated with the doctor. It was very unpleasant. It's impossible to keep it a secret. She has to stay in bed for three days. It has to go through Munk. Her mother was upset at first, but afterward she behaved fabulously, very understandingly. She didn't blame anybody. She spoke to Jirka as though nothing had happened, just told him how stupid he was. Two days later the confirmation came from public health. Since she's found out, she's been feeling better. She just looks terrible, and we talk every evening until late at night. It's no small matter. Won't it have consequences for the rest of her life? I think I'd be unhappy, and then what about Mommy! I told her about it to see where she stands. She's totally convinced that she can rely on me and that I'd never do anything like that. I didn't talk to her about it anymore. If I got into that kind of a situation, I wouldn't let Mommy find out about it. And it's not out of the question. Today Eva, tomorrow maybe me. I could never disappoint Mommy like that. It would be a terrible blow for her. Thursday on the eleventh I went to the hospital with Eva. I've been with Otto in the attic a few more times.

Seven thousand more people will be sent away within the week. Who knows if one of us won't be among them? How long will we remain together? Many people knew they were in it by Saturday. By Sunday everything was definite. Mommy had to move out of the Hamburg. The sluice took place there. At first they said she'd have to go to the attic. We packed her things with Otto. But it turned out she only had to go next door to the nurses' room. Everybody went to the sluice on Sunday. The transport left on Monday. Some of us are doing voluntary service. We helped people carry luggage. This time it was well organized. We were able to help them all the way to the train. Otto has found out he may be in the next transport. The organization protecting him up to now will probably send him because he's young and doesn't have a family. I might volunteer to go with him. He won't allow it. What should I do? He's not ambivalent about it either. He goes to the doctor every day. But if they send him, he'll go.

Eva was operated on. I was there twice a day with Jirka. Eva's taking it superbly, not a word of blame. Two days later she found out she's in the second transport, the one that's leaving on Tuesday. Otto found out in the meantime that he's probably not in the transport, but his doctor and family are. Daddy and Otto go to the Magdeburg every day. The transport's being changed all the time. What if one of us is in it? My parents are pretty secure because of Daddy's medal, but they're worried for me. Somehow I feel secure too. I carried luggage all day Tuesday, until four in the afternoon. By then all the people were in the trains with their luggage. The Taussigs and a group of people from the farm waited for the third transport, but they've got no hope of being pulled out. It had been put together by Tuesday afternoon. Could we possibly be so lucky that none of us is directly affected by it? I meet Daddy at night. He's upset: "You're in it." I was completely calm. Nobody I told it to wanted to believe it. Mommy arrived without knowing a thing. She nearly had a heart attack. Mommy and Daddy are terribly upset. Otto turned white as chalk, quickly lit a cigarette, and went to his mother to tell her he was going with me. Everybody in the Družstvo was informed. There was terrible chaos everywhere. New lists were made again. Everybody who was in and got out is in again. I have a very low number and no reserve, so almost no hope of being pulled out. Fixler tried to at least get us all into the reserve. If even he can't give us any hope! Mommy slept with me. We packed all night. Four girls helped me until one. I was given my classification Wednesday morning. I went to Otto's at six. He's very upset and went to the Družstvo. I'll have to report at noon. I still had some packing to do in the morning and took care of some other things. A big relief. I'm going with the entire Löbl family. If anybody's going to have connections again, it's the Löbls. Karel won't let us down. I got five thousand crowns from them.

Otto and I went to see his mother in the morning. Of course she's against it. How could a mother think otherwise? I completely agreed with her. He shouldn't go with me. Otto's torn. He loves his mother very much but doesn't want me to go alone. When Otto asked for advice, he was told that without him, his mother would no longer be protected and would probably be pulled into the transport automatically. That was a determining factor. Though he hasn't made up his mind yet, it's almost certain he won't go. I'm talking myself into believing it's better that way. He has to stay with his mother. It's a terribly difficult decision for my parents to stay. Mommy would much rather go than stay here. Daddy and I had a hard time talking her out of it, saying she'd only be a burden for me, it would be very selfish of her to go, and Daddy needs her here. Finally she let herself be talked out of it. It must have been a horrible decision for her, though she didn't show it. I'm calm all the time. When you're in the middle of it, you're not conscious of it at all. It's much worse for people who still have doubts and don't know what they should do.

Emka, our group leader, went with me to see Gerson, Ziegler, and Fixler several times. She won't let go. "You can't let our best worker go." Otto doesn't say a word; he just keeps looking at me. And I try to distract him by giving him all kinds of work. At noon I turn in my meal card, points, and money. Then I register and report in. A hundred farewells. "Farewell until Prague."

Daddy is in the Magdeburg day and night, running from one place to the next, trying to get me out. He won't let go. He finds people everywhere who are truly concerned. Everybody knows him and knows that his only daughter, his only happiness, is in the transport and he won't survive her departure. He's miserably unhappy. Mommy doesn't speak, just packs and kisses me once in a while. She has tears in her eyes and only talks about what still needs to be done and what I still need. We're lucky Mommy lives in the Hamburg and has a pass. Otto, Mommy, and I use it all the time to get in and out. At times I have the transport number around my neck, at others the pass in hand, and at still others the white transport administration band, whatever I need at the time. That's how we spent the afternoon. Then at about five Daddy came in, screaming, "She's out!" We ran up and down, laughing and crying. I still don't believe it, but they told Daddy in the Magdeburg. I ran to the Družstvo, but nobody knew anything about it there. I went to see Helenka, who's become quite a good friend. She already knew. The three of us are on the list of people who were pulled out. Schliesser showed it to Trude Jolisch. I still don't dare to believe it. It would be too beautiful. Otto comes and just caresses me. He hadn't lost hope. We walked around as though in a dream. Mommy's still very upset. Rahm stands in the yard with hundreds of people making a pilgrimage to him to tell him their woes. He'd like to get them all out of the transport. He listens to everybody and actually does answer some of their pleas. The order suddenly came at six: "Take your places. Everybody must be present for Rahm." What's going to happen to those of us who were pulled out? He couldn't possibly put us back in. And then what? I went to Gerson to find out. He didn't know either. There seems to be a completely new order, and the list of people pulled out is probably no longer valid. We all have to go report. An unsettling moment. We were almost the first. "What work do you do?" he asked. "Farming." "Where?" "In the garden." "Outside." I was sent to the row of those who were pulled out. Everybody's congratulating me. Is it really over and final? Nobody knows. Most of the young people capable of working got off free. Whoever said farming was released. A lot of people got off. It lasted forever until they were finally through. Of course there was lots of swindling going on. Certain people went past Rahm four or five times in the hope they'd be released, or they'd stare into the swarm toward a table of people who were pulled out. And there was no end, and there was no end. We stood there from six to twelve.

It's a terrible feeling to see the fate of thousands of people dependent on a single person, and how in a matter of seconds he judges each individual's fate. It seems like a mass judgment to me: life or death. Just according to your face. Gerson stood next to Rahm from ten with the list from the farm. When one of us came up, he would say to Rahm, "He's on the list," where-upon Rahm would say: "Outside," or, "He's not on the list," and then, "Go on," and he was in the transport, so actually Rahm wasn't presiding over us anymore but rather Gerson. It was an unbelievable move on his part, and it took a lot of courage. It also took a completely pure, unprejudiced conscience, and Gerson has that.

It must have looked like a giant theater: the yard light as day with floodlights, a huge queue of people, and Rahm in the middle. He divides two groups of people, one beaming with joy, the other desperately unhappy. The former group re-mained standing in the yard in rows of six. It was finally over at twelve.

What's going to happen now? A tense moment. We could barely stand at this point, and only nervous tension kept us on our feet. All the balconies surrounding the yard were filled to the brim with people watching this vast drama. I saw my parents standing up there with Otto. I was the very first one in the first row. "Everybody step forward again." Before I knew what was happening, I was in front of Rahm, who asked me the same question again and added: "Alone?" "Yes, alone." "Well, then, over here." And I was back in a row. It was divided once more. Only this time nobody knew who was outside and who wasn't.

We went through yet another horrible hour of uncertainty. Dead tired. We stood in two rows, each with approximately the same number of people, all of them strong, healthy, and young. Very few families. What will they do with us? One person thought that they'd make it a worker transport, another that they'd breed another race with us. It was over at two. The most tense hour of the night. Epstein went over to the other group and told them something. Rahm was also nervous by then and bellowed like a bull, threatening them with blows. Then Epstein came up to us and said, "Everybody here has been taken out of the transport. You'll get the confirmation tomorrow. In the event you are erroneously put into the transport, you should notify me instantly." I have no idea how I got to my bed. Margit woke me at five: "You're in the reserve; get dressed right away." At first I was horrified. What's that supposed to mean? Mommy started to cry. I calmed her down. "I'm out for sure; it must be a mistake." On the way I found out that all of us who were out got numbers from seven thousand to eight thousand, and the reserve with numbers over eight thousand were put in. So we're out. I ran to tell Otto. He was in the Magdeburg with his brother until five. I told him I was one hundred percent out. They're already drafting the confirmations that we'll be getting in the course of the day.

Löbl visited Mommy at night. He told her that as my mother, she shouldn't allow me to meet Karel. He's very worried about him. I walk around in a daze. I still can't figure it out. I got my confirmation in the morning and helped the transport all afternoon. I brought the Taussigs' luggage all the way to the train. Poor Eva. She's so unhappy. Jirka doesn't care about her at all anymore. He didn't even come to say good-bye. Trude Jolisch left with her mother too. I lay down in the afternoon. Otto was with me the whole time, caressing me, kissing my hands. We're terribly happy. At night we had a festive dinner, cans of ham and wine. Mommy had night duty, and I stayed with Otto in the Hamburg. It was risky. You're supposed to sign out, but others stayed too. I stayed in a small room overnight. I'm so happy.

1944

Theresienstadt is bursting with improvements. They're expecting a commission and doing the most unbelievable things. We had to work all day Sunday. After the first raptures were over, I quickly got used to normal life again and was only silently happy. There are masses of lettuce. It's delivered two days a week at five in the morning. We're getting rations of it too, and there's plenty to go around. Beautification consists of fixing up the grounds. All free areas are being planted with lawns, partly even with flowers; benches are being set up everywhere. The Ring Square is especially beautiful. It has a music pavillion where there will be concerts every night. The curfew has been extended to ten. A pavillion that defies description has been put up in the nursery: a big paddle pond, lots of toys, delightful baby beds; only they're locked up and guarded by a ghetto guard. Sokol Hall is being newly refurbished: beautiful furniture is being brought in, and they'll hold lectures and give concerts and plays there. They're setting up tables and chairs in the streets with colorful umbrellas, a library with good books, a restaurant with every amenity. An entire barracks had to be evacuated within two hours for the latter. There are tables with white tablecloths, waiters and waitresses with white caps and aprons, roasted potatoes with onions, cucumber salad, and plates with cutlery, but it's all for two days before the commission to two days after it. The food is more abundant and better: vegetables and, for dinner, soup, potatoes, and a roll. For all of that, the food was worse a month before and will be a month after, too. Kurzawe's villa has been evacuated and a nursery for sick children set up.

JUNE 23, FRIDAY: The commission arrived at noon. We all had to show up well dressed with rakes and picks, cheerfully singing on rack wagons. We met the commission on the way. It was made up of about ten men: Danes, Swedes, and supposedly the director of the Swiss Red Cross. The Fascists were also supposed to be present. Epstein showed them around, and Rahm walked behind them, smiling sweetly. The gentlemen were apparently quite skeptical and didn't believe by any stretch the things they were seeing. Thank God. It's all such a hideous show. All Theresienstadt was talking about it of course. Children were apparently trained to hug Rahm in the street and say: "Come play with us, Uncle Rahm." And he'd reply, "Sorry, dear children, I'm too busy today. Tomorrow, maybe." Then he'd pull a can of sardines from his pocket: "Sardines again?" And lots of other such farces. Vostrel drove Epstein in his car.

JUNE–JULY: There was an invasion on June 8 by British and American forces in France near Cherbourg. The Germans were prepared for them, and fighting is heaviest there. The allies have conquered a narrow strip of the coast. Offensives are being launched on the Eastern front and in Italy simultaneously. They're advancing on all fronts. For the last two weeks, I've been getting newspapers and food from Karel daily. He's finally come to his senses and agrees it's better if we don't meet. I got cream, eggs, meat, and fat almost every day. A courier came from Birkenau during the commission. We got news from Mama, Lotte, and Egon Samek. Good news from Lotte, not so good from Mama and Egon. I wrote to Lotte's friend in Prague to see whether he knows if Mama and Lotte are together and if he's sending packages to Mama. I often get sardines now.

I have a big problem. Otto wants to get married. He's terribly sensitive, and I don't want to upset him. He's tired all the time lately and doesn't feel well, and it puts him in a bad mood. I've become friends with his family. I'm terribly afraid our relationship will not remain without consequences.

I really want to move. I can't stand the barracks any longer with all the bugs. We sleep on the ground between the barracks every night. It's a catastrophe when it rains. Some people have comfortable rooms; married people live together luxuriously; others are squeezed together with thousands of bugs. Some don't know what to do with all the food they have; others suffer from tuberculosis, osteomalacia, and anemia that come from poor nutrition and are increasing frighteningly. The enormous differences are quite typical of the ghetto. But you can't get frantic; you can't let it get the better of you.

JULY 16, SUNDAY: I can't remember having had such a gorgeous birthday. Saturday night we celebrated it at my parents'. The beautiful things I got covered an entire table: laundry bags in all sizes, containers for toiletries, a small cupboard, a purse, wooden shoes, a cake, two scarves, a sweater, a box of chocolate candies from Karel (though unknowingly). Then I went to see Otto, certain he knew nothing. He played along. Then I went to my place and almost fell from the ladder. A giant bouquet of roses and carnations, a cake, a box of sweets, perfume. I was beside myself. Otto grinned, his surprise a success. I went to the Ravellin [guards' room] alone next to the sheep stall. Sunday was a normal work day. At night I went back to the Ravellin. Eight girls wanting to sleep there too came at ten. All of a sudden a ghetto guard remembered that we're not allowed to sleep there. After much toing and froing it was now eleven; by then we had to move out. The Domestic Affairs Office didn't approve it, but our bosses Gerson and Kurzawe gave their approval for us to sleep there, and that's what counts. We were accompanied by a ghetto guard to the Magdeburg. They didn't know anything about it there. Only Epstein could give us a permit. So we went to see Epstein. He wasn't in. Only Murmelstein was there. He consulted with Zucker. Zucker listened to everything and thought it over, then Schliesser came and a few other big shots and they all consulted about it. They were sorry, they said, but we'd have to leave that night. The others were asleep by the time we came back. We packed our blankets and moved into the Družstvo. Gerson allowed us to sleep in the office. We didn't sleep much, but we laughed a lot. I'll never forget how nine heaps of misery wandered through Theresienstadt in our blankets, some with hair curlers. When we got to the Družstvo, a window opened and a sleepy voice said, "Coming for the equipment?" The old coot didn't even forget his duty at night. Then we sat at the pond for a long while in the moonlight and just laughed. It was a funny end to my birthday.

JULY 17, MONDAY: We've had a huge blow. Heindl has taken over the supervision of the farm. He's the worst boss imaginable and started off with a bang: he had two people thrown into jail the first day. The second day there was another row, and on the third day he extended work to eleven hours. He watched us from behind a tree in the garden on the first day of our new extended hours, and when he saw four girls sit down, he raced across the garden on his motorcycle like a madman and made them work fourteen hours. They had to put the garden into impeccable order. He wouldn't release them any earlier either. He's just impossible. Three other groups got the same punishment simultaneously and came back from work between seven to ten at night. It wasn't a week before Heindl came and turned the entire garden on its head. He ransacked everything, crawled all over the floor, and found some vegetables, just a few, but enough for him to punish the entire garden. Every night we have to work from eight to nine besides our normal work hours. When he saw Isi, our group leader, he walked straight up to him and started yelling questions at him, like what he does here every night after eleven, where he takes the wheelbarrow with cucumbers, what he does in the warehouse at night? In short he seemed very well informed. He slapped him after every word. Anyone else would have keeled over after the first slap; Isi just bled. Finally he threw Isi in the pool. Isi's been fired from the garden and has to work eighteen hours a day now, from 3:30 in the morning to 10 at night, but he'll be able to take it.

A new worry is that all the officers have to be registered. It's generally believed that they're going to be sent to an internment camp at Zell near Hamburg. Daddy too. I don't know what I should do. I was convinced from the first that I'd go with them, but Otto talked me out of it and is terribly unhappy. My parents are also convinced I should stay. I really don't know what to do.

The Russians have taken Lemberg, Lublin, Brest, Litewsk, and according to local reports, they're even farther along than that. The mood here is very hopeful. Is the end near?

I'm always dead tired after work from six to eleven, one to seven, and eight to nine and can barely stand on my feet. On top of it all, sleeping in the barracks is hideous. I haven't slept for around two months now. It's crawling with bugs there during the day, not to mention at night.

Sleeping outside isn't bad; it's just that right now it's so rainy, we can't. I usually sleep at Mommy's when she's got night duty, but this constant toing and froing is unpleasant. I can hardly get any reading or studying done and can make it to English no more than once a week. I badly want to move, but have few prospects. Otto has none either. Everything's all right with Karel, but Otto's very against it, and I had a very heated debate with him. I suddenly came down with a fever of over 100°F one day. Probably from the sun. But where can I lie down? Just in the Hamburg. I had to report sick and was laid up for five days. During that time they deloused the barracks. I had to go to the attic in the Dresden. The attic is horrible. It's so hot you could die, and then the bugs, thousands of them. The delousing lasted for ten days.

I've gone back to work. We have a new boss. An older man, very decent and reasonable, who doesn't cause any unnecessary problems. He's an expert and knows exactly what he wants.

A work transport has been called for August 22. Three people from the farm were made available. Two of them were pulled out, and Otto was put in. His lot was drawn. I immediately ran to Gerson. Unfortunately he can't do anything about the lottery. I went to Rahm in the afternoon and was received while he was being examined by the doctor. I've packed everything up meanwhile. Otto had to move to the Jäger barracks that same afternoon. I lugged everything up to the attic of the Hamburg because his barracks were being fumigated. We had to break the news gently to his mother. Otto's brother did everything he could in the Magdeburg, but there's little hope.

Everybody congratulated me at work in the morning. He's out. Crazy. How so? Gerson has confirmed it. Epstein called at night: Kellner's out. Only he didn't know where Otto lived. Otto couldn't believe it. He came to pick me up at noon. He was out. But now he's back in again. Gerson is suddenly involved in the case. He went with Otto to see Epstein. I waited outside. Epstein could give him little hope. The list is in Prague by now, and nobody can do anything at the moment. After much effort Otto's brother has managed to get him X-rayed. He feels stomach ulcers are a good enough reason to get him off. Meanwhile, I had to sit in delousing all morning. It's an awful procedure. You're bathed while all your things and towels are deloused. You have to sit there in a borrowed nightgown for three hours. I ran to the Hamburg, still wearing the nightgown. They found an ulcer in the X ray. It was an old one but still there. We have a little hope again.

We went to Reinisch with the news, but he wouldn't accept it. He said Otto was able to do light work. Garden work is considered relatively light work, and if he can do it here, he can do it anywhere. Reinisch is smooth as an eel, very friendly, and easy to talk to. I don't know why everybody's so afraid of him, though most likely he won't do anything. He promised to present it to Rahm again.

We went back to Gerson one more time and thanked him for his trouble, even though it was unfortunately all for nothing. "What do you mean, for nothing? Come with me." He grabbed both of us and we went to Reinisch. Doctor Weiss had to come too. He had to give him somebody as a replacement and said Reinisch would give his consent if the person was declared healthy and more capable than Otto. We're getting somewhere if Reinisch makes promises to Gerson. We then went to see the person from work headquarters who organized everything. We only got to his wife. Gerson explained that we were very interested in keeping Otto here and that he didn't want to tear us apart either. She had to understand.

We went back to the Magdeburg at ten, and Gerson repeated his entire story. We got home at eleven and didn't want to get our hopes up. Doctor Weiss was at Reinisch's until one. I went to Gerson's in the morning, and he had a very dubious expression on his face. A new complication had arisen. They called for the replacement but couldn't find him. All the ghetto guards were alarmed. They were notified of a possible escape attempt. The people were found in the morning, but it was too late. They were supposed to be at Rahm's by 7:30 A.M. Of all things at the last moment!

Nobody was at work in headquarters in the morning. So back to Gerson. Kurzawe promised to speak to Rahm again. Back to the Magdeburg. Otto took his place in the lineup. I went to S. He was very decent: He was so sorry, but there's very little hope. The boys had to be standing in front of Rahm at headquarters. Out of sheer desperation I went through the blockade and back to Epstein and asked if there was any hope. He was very sorry, but there was nothing to be done. The replacement offered by the farm wasn't good enough. So even though he was out last night, he had to be put back in. My last ray of hope was gone. All our efforts were for nothing.

Everybody had to line up in front of Rahm. Dr. Reinisch was called when they got to Otto. He said something to him, and Otto was told to go behind the others and stand alone. What does it mean? Will he perhaps have to . . . ? S. stood next to me and said, all excited, "Kellner's out. We have to send a replacement for a gardener." Then he squeezed my hand. Another five were pulled out of the lineup. They all had to stand there a long time. Rahm spoke to them first, then Epstein. The people in the transport were then released. Rahm looked over the people he pulled out of the transport. A miracle has occurred. Otto is out, and I am lying in his arms.

AUGUST: The situation has changed drastically in a single month. It's almost impossible to believe how successful the British have been. Since the June invasion, they have intervened in a flash, marching from France to Belgium and completely occupying Belgium in three days, Holland within a few more days, and in the following week, all of France except for a few exceptions. Americans are being shipped out of the south of France, which they have occupied, and gone over the Alps into Italy. The Russians have occupied Romania and Bulgaria in the east. There's been an uprising in Slovakia. The rebels have occupied a large part of the country except for Pressburg. The Russians have reached the Carpathians and are supposedly also in Slovakia. In short, I can hardly believe it. The British have broken through the Siegfried Line at various points and are expected to cross the Rhein in the next few days. They apparently already have Aachen. The effect of these events on the ghetto is enormous. People are happy. There are joyous faces everywhere. There are air raid warnings twice a day. The allies seem to be flying from Belgium and France. Brünn and Pardubitz have supposedly been bombarded. You can clearly see large squadrons of foreign airplanes.

SEPTEMBER: The Germans are conceding a lot. They're in a very, very serious predicament. Kurzawe held a meeting. He said he hoped that since we'd managed to get along so well for so long, things weren't going to change now. He said he probably wouldn't have another chance to speak to us and we shouldn't let ourselves be misguided by people from outside and driven to rash acts that could be our ruin.

Epstein gave a speech with approximately the same content, just more heartfelt. He begged us several times, "in the interest of everyone here," that we bear with him these last moments and stay calm. He said that it would be false heroics for irresponsible people to believe they had to do something for their liberation; that would be totally wrong, and even the smallest incident could mean the ruin of all Theresienstadt. He compared us to a ship close to port, but a port surrounded by mines. Only the captain knew the way. It might be a roundabout way, but he would bring us safely to port. The crew heard voices from the port beckoning them, encouraging them to come. The crew was impatient and couldn't wait to dock, yet waiting was the only thing to do.

That's the theory, but the question is how it would be put into practice. I doubt that certain people can be stopped by such speeches and don't know what's right.

Otto and I were with the Gersons over the holidays. Gerson was very happy, chatted for a long time, and even took a present from us without being insulted, which was something we'd feared. The holidays were celebrated with more joy this year than in the past. The mood is such that any day could be the end. I imagine we'll be here for a few more months, but what happens to us then is a big question mark, and I can't say I'm very optimistic.

Work is still the same. We still smuggle all the time, and Heindl cannot talk us out of it. Lately, though, he hasn't been with us. He's taken over the mica-manufacturing barracks. The poor mica workers.

■   ■   ■

I have a big problem with Otto. He insists on getting married and has talked to Mommy about it. Mommy's against it. She doesn't want me to rush things. Otto's extraordinarily good and decent. He is immensely fond of me and wants to give me everything I could possibly desire. I would never be alone again. Then again, he's a farmer, a profession I have nothing in common with. He's not very educated and isn't energetic or ambitious. I don't dare compare him to Richard. If I left Otto, he'd be terribly unhappy. But I want to wait. In any case, I've asked him to give me some leeway, and he's agreed to give me time to think about it and won't talk about it. But for how long?

I haven't heard from Karel in over a month. Could something have happened?

If I were to try very hard, I could probably get a better place to live for some food and a few cigarettes. But then I think it's not really worth it.

Maybe I'm too comfortable to set up a place. There's a lot of running around and work involved. If I complain about my living conditions, I only have myself to blame. Helena is building a nice garret room. Otto has no such possibility. He has very few vegetables and gives them to his mother or trades them for medicine. I visit Otto's mother often. I give her whatever vegetables and food I can. Even though I've got a lot of everything, it almost isn't enough for all the friends who need it.

WRITTEN ON MAY 19, 1965: *My diary breaks off for four months at this point. As so often before, the transports destroyed everything.*

One transport after another relentlessly left for Poland in October. In contrast to earlier transports, there were no reprieves, no appeals, no summons, no pardons possible. The inhabitants of Theresienstadt were divided into categories, and each transport had its own designated category. There were transports with young people or old people, transports for officers and Jews who had war honors, transports for council elders, and so on. Whoever fell into the category went. The farm remained protected, so I stayed to the end, utterly alone.

Otto was the first to leave, in October, then Gerson, then my parents. I volunteered to go, went to Rahm and begged to be allowed to go with my parents. But all for nought. I remained condemned to life, and to life in Theresienstadt.

I was totally destroyed and apathetic. My life had no meaning, my diary had no meaning. I stopped writing.

Karel Kosvanec continued to support me. After Löbl was sent to Poland, other members of the group mediated my contacts with him, people of far lesser stature than Löbl, more black marketeers than adventurers. But even they were for the most part sent to Poland.

Karel asked me to maintain my relationship with him. I did. On every moonless night I waited for him near the barbed wire behind Sokol Hall and witnessed his courage and his nearly supernatural instinct for danger.

He traveled along a brook lined with overgrown shrubs to the two powerful bastions of the old fortress, where guards stood with machine guns and searchlights. The last few yards consisted of a steep incline up to the tangles of barbed wire. Karel ue use of every shadow, every dark spot. He was able to crawl soundlessly on all fours for endless periods. He could lie motionless for hours just yards away from the barbed wire and wipe away his every trail in the snow behind him.

It would often be close to two in the morning when he finally arrived, bringing a hundred-pound sack, a package for me, and a letter. He would take the package of gold and money I'd received from Pacovsky, say a few brief words or give me instructions, and disappear again into the dark. I would lug the heavy sack to Frau Fantl's tiny room in the cellar of Sokol Hall, where we sorted the contents of the sack into small packages. The next day we would deliver them inconspicuously to the recipients.

It was an unnerving double life for me, meeting Karel at night and by day working on the farm. I led it without joy, satisfaction, or any profit for myself; I led it out of gratitude to Karel and because I didn't care about living anymore.

I started my diary again in January, but by then it was merely a register of events of the final days. Nothing was so important that I wanted to keep it in my memory, nothing so personal that I wanted to confide it to a diary.

1945

JANUARY 1, MONDAY: Two transports from Slovakia. Women and children were half frozen.

JANUARY 14, SUNDAY: Huge incident. A bunch of cigarettes found. Twenty-one people arrested. The whole ghetto threatened with severe punishment. Worried about Karel.

JANUARY 15, MONDAY: Confinement to barracks. Starting Wednesday, no light or heat if the person associating with the Aryan isn't found. Karel here again.

JANUARY 16, TUESDAY: Will the people involved confess by tomorrow?

JANUARY 17, WEDNESDAY: The Aryans have been found. They're SS. All punishments canceled. Karel passed over.

JANUARY 18, THURSDAY: Russian offensive on the whole front. New tanks on sleds. A new fluid has been invented to render the military powerless.

JANUARY 19, FRIDAY: Two transports from Slovakia.

JANUARY 20, SATURDAY: The Russians have taken Cracow, Kattowitz, Lodz, and apparently Breslau and are advancing toward Berlin. Our people may have been liberated.

JANUARY 23, TUESDAY: A row of blocks had to be evacuated within twenty-four hours. Everybody moved to the Holland. Barracks being built day and night on the citadel. They must be expecting big transports, but from where?

JANUARY 26, FRIDAY: I take Frau Kellner a quart of milk every day. Though it's risky, she enjoys it.

JANUARY 30, TUESDAY: The Russians have crossed the Oder. They're just sixty-two miles from Berlin.

JANUARY 31, WEDNESDAY: A thousand people have arrived from Prague, the Jewish half of mixed marriages. They were in jail in Prague at Hagibor, where they did forced labor. Nobody I knew. They were in the sluice at night. They had cigarettes and money taken from them in large quantities.

FEBRUARY 1, THURSDAY: Lots of transports every day from all parts of Germany and the Sudetenland. Lots of the Jews from mixed marriages.

FEBRUARY 2, FRIDAY: Waited for Karel, but he didn't come.

FEBRUARY 3, SATURDAY: The Russians are supposed to be in Berlin, Ostrau, Náchod. A thousand people are rumored to be leaving for Switzerland on Monday. Some people really believe it. Most don't.

FEBRUARY 4, SUNDAY: The Prague transport came. I was called but turned it down. It seems voluntary. Frau Fantl is going. Crazy. I helped her pack at night. Karel came here at night. I can't imagine the next transport's going to Switzerland. It's too fantastic.

FEBRUARY–MARCH: Magnificent trains arrived for the transport. Can it really be going to Switzerland? Won't I regret it? I don't care about me alone. Frau Fantl left me with lots of things to take care of. Karel came at night.

FEBRUARY 7, WEDNESDAY: Karel again. It's horrible to walk through Theresienstadt at night, lugging things and always wondering where to go with them.

FEBRUARY 8, THURSDAY: Got a garret from Pacovsky where I can leave the things.

FEBRUARY 10, SATURDAY: Daily transports from Germany. All mixed marriages have been separated. Prague transport arrived.

FEBRUARY 11, SUNDAY: Two hundred boys came from Germany. The entire barracks construction crew and a couple of girls. Nobody expected they'd still be coming.

FEBRUARY 12, MONDAY: Some of the boys were locked up under police surveillance. Many of the women are happy to have their husbands there.

FEBRUARY 13, TUESDAY: Karel's here every night. I haven't slept and am nervous.

FEBRUARY 14, WEDNESDAY: Herr Kohn and his brothers came from Prague. Karel's new friend Emmi Schmied came with me tonight.

FEBRUARY 15, THURSDAY: Karel's last time. Finally. I breathed a sigh of relief. I can't do it anymore.

FEBRUARY 16, FRIDAY: The Russians are very close to Berlin. Dresden is completely destroyed. Every day trains carrying fugitives travel in the direction of Reichenberg.

FEBRUARY 18, SUNDAY: A barrack burned down. Shoe repair shops. Lots of thrashing and as a consequence, no heat for all Theresienstadt.

FEBRUARY 19, MONDAY: A big aerial attack on Prague. Supposedly two thousand are dead.

FEBRUARY 20, TUESDAY: Reichenberg and Dresden evacuated. Every day there are streams of fugitives in terrible condition passing through Theresienstadt on foot and in wagons, cars, and trains.

FEBRUARY 22, THURSDAY: Seven people have arrived from Litzmannstadt. They were on foot for twenty days. Nobody was allowed to talk to them. They were shut off completely at the citadel.

FEBRUARY 24, FRIDAY: Daily transports from Germany. All without stars. Privileged marriages.

FEBRUARY 26, MONDAY: Prague transport. Mr. Glaser.

FEBRUARY 27, TUESDAY: The Prague people feel superior and are unhappy here. Nothing's good enough for them, and they feel terribly sorry for themselves.

MARCH 2, FRIDAY: Turkey is at war with Germany.

■　　　■　　　■

MARCH 4, SUNDAY: Karel came. I told him we can't meet so often. He's angry. He wrote a six-page letter.

MARCH 8, MONDAY: Karel doesn't want to come anymore. I don't care.

MARCH 12, MONDAY: Karel came. Spoke only to Emmi. They're busy building more barracks.

MARCH 13, TUESDAY: New transports are arriving every day from Slovakia and Hungary. You hear all sorts of languages. Very little Czech.

MARCH 13, WEDNESDAY: Went to see Karel with Emmi.

MARCH 15, THURSDAY: Karel at night again. Am at my wits' end. Went alone. There was a light burning all night. Worked all night. Breathed a sigh of relief.

MARCH 16, FRIDAY: There will probably be light again. Very happy. Went at night again. Dark. Karel was waiting. Suddenly there was light again. A quick couple of words. He apologized. Brought twenty-eight hundred cigarettes.

MARCH 19, MONDAY: Every day there are from one to three air raid alarms. Each time hundreds of planes fly over Theresienstadt. Work constantly disrupted.

MARCH 20, TUESDAY: All Theresienstadt is standing on its head clearing things out and giving the place a thorough cleaning. A medical commission is expected.

■   ■   ■

MARCH 21, WEDNESDAY: The cows need very little work. We lie in the sun a lot and tan. The weather is magnificent.

MARCH 22, THURSDAY: Lots of milk is being smuggled. We're not allowed to work anymore at lunch. Our German supervisor is with us the entire time, and yet . . .

MARCH 23, FRIDAY: We're working one and a half hours in the morning and one and a half hours in the afternoon, while others work the entire day. We're allowed to leave with any vehicle we like and can go wherever we want. Freiberger was put into jail; nobody knows why.

MARCH 24, SATURDAY: Corpses are being buried now, not burned.

MARCH 25, SUNDAY: They're prettying things up here again: they're expecting a foreign commission. Magnificent displays of goods. Headquarters is being remodeled into a Jewish office.

MARCH 26, MONDAY: The British are advancing quickly. They've crossed the Rhein at several points.

MARCH 27, TUESDAY: The Russians have occupied several villages in the Sudetenland. They're fighting for Ostrau.

MARCH 28, WEDNESDAY: Freiberger's free again. Nobody knows why he was in jail.

MARCH 29, TUESDAY: All pictures in Theresienstadt have to be stamped. Photographs of people who are gone aren't allowed on the walls. The mood is that the war will be over any day now. Theresienstadt is delirious with joy. It hardly touches me at all.

APRIL 4, WEDNESDAY: Went to Karel with Emmi and Vera. A policeman suddenly appeared and wanted to know what we were doing. He searched us and found nothing. I had gold and three thousand cigarettes on me. We had to go to headquarters. In the end we talked him out of it, and he let us go.

APRIL 5, THURSDAY: The commission came in the morning in beautiful trucks with chocolate, rice, and cheese. We grabbed two pounds of sugar, three cheeses, and forty pounds of rice. There was chocolate for children and adults.

APRIL 6, FRIDAY: The commission drove around all day in their cars. They looked at everything and left at night. Karel wrote. He's expecting us this evening near Sokol Hall. Franta cheerfully came with us. I'm very glad. Maybe he'll take over.

People placed lots of hope in the commission, saying it would either stay or take us with them. None of it came true. All backpacks had to be turned in. We're not giving anything up of course.

APRIL 8, SUNDAY: Forty men are leaving to build barracks again, most of them closely related to Aryans, but others too.

Pressburg and parts of Vienna have been occupied.

APRIL 9, MONDAY: Went to Karel with Franta at night. Everything's fine. It's much better with Franta than with the women. Gave the things to the Hamburg and got home at eleven.

APRIL 10, TUESDAY: Franta went to Karel's alone tonight. Then he came to me. Everything worked out well. Five people have escaped. They're keeping everything under strict control.

APRIL 11, WEDNESDAY: Six miles from Bremen, forty-three miles from Nürnberg. Königsberg fell on Tuesday. Žilina too, apparently. All German women and children have been evacuated from Prague. Ten people escaped. There's lots of contact with Aryans everywhere.

APRIL 12, THURSDAY: The third barracks construction transport has left. Mostly mixed marriages. Seven men left from here. They've intensified surveillance. Nobody's allowed outside after nine.

APRIL 13, FRIDAY: An order came suddenly at five for all Danes to go to the sluice. They're going to Sweden. Great jubilation. No control at night. Went to Karel with Franta.

APRIL 14, SATURDAY: Eight white buses with red crosses came. The Swedish drivers talked to everybody. They brought lots of cigarettes. They were led home, accompanied by music and the envy of thousands.

APRIL 16, MONDAY: Franta, Maria, and Frau Kellner visited me tonight.

APRIL 18, WEDNESDAY: Large-scale Russian and American offensive close to Berlin. The two fronts connecting between Leipzig and Dresden. Vienna in Russian hands.

An alarm sounded suddenly at night: "We're free!" All Theresienstadt is delirious. Everybody's hugging each other, singing hymns. Rahm called a meeting and pleaded for calm. Murmelstein denied everything. "We're not under the Red Cross. Everything's as usual. It was lucky there wasn't any shooting." The Germans are preparing to depart. All papers have been burned, all rations and valuable items were confiscated. Six hundred people with relatives in Switzerland are to go there.

APRIL 22, SUNDAY: Everyone wants to go to Switzerland. Everybody's looking for contacts. Only children with parents outside or people with verifiable visas or foreigners can go. It's a complete fraud. All the bigwigs are going too.

APRIL–MAY: A large transport from every possible concentration camp arrived in the afternoon, about two thousand men and women in hideous shape—starving and parched. They look horrible. Lots of Polish men and eighty women from the last transport. Magda, Lidka, and Nita Petschau are almost unrecognizable after their release. Emaciated to the bone, racked with fever, striped uniforms, shaved heads. Lidka was taken to the hospital. She couldn't stand. Most had to be carried. They told us gruesome things.

At nine in the evening all the boys returned from barracks construction. They were away for a week. Many Aryans were among them and dangerous criminals who've never known a normal life. We've got all that here now.

APRIL 26, THURSDAY: Every day hundreds of men and women arrive from all the concentration camps, mostly by foot. Two hundred girls from the last group were in relatively better condition than the rest. A few of the men there are from here. Otherwise they're from Poland and Hungary and have spent three to four years in the camps and look horrible. The women are in somewhat better shape. I'm helping as a nurse with the transports. All of them have temperatures. They have diarrhea when they eat even the smallest amount of food. They're covered with lice, and all of them are suspected to have typhoid. A member of the Swiss Red Cross has taken over and assured us he'll take care of us and make certain we're safe. Almost everybody from Birkenau is telling the most unbelievable things. Men and women were separated immediately after arrival. Everyone was undressed, and the SS selected a small group to stay in a barracks surrounded by an electric wire for about a week. From there they were put into different prison camps. The others were probably gassed. They can see the smoke and flames from people burning day and night. Sick people, but also healthy people, old people, children with mothers. Entire transports with no distinction.

APRIL 30, MONDAY: The last battles for Berlin. It's two-thirds occupied. Hitler is dying. Mussolini has been executed. All the Germans are escaping from the Protectorate.

MAY 1, TUESDAY: Daily duty in the hospital. Lidka was brought to the Hohenelber. It's a horrible job. Everybody's full of lice. Waited for Karel at the train station with Franta until midnight. Went to the Dresden with the paper. He wanted to come into the ghetto. Went to Emmi. Somebody spoke to me on the way back. It was Karel. He'd gone to a different place than we'd arranged. He climbed over the fence. He stayed until 2:30.

MAY 3, THURSDAY: Karel came again the next day. I showed him everything. He's by no means the only Aryan here. Lots of Aryan halves of mixed marriages came. People are leaving every night. I'm supposed to go too.

MAY 4, FRIDAY: Is it possible it's really over? Simply unbelievable. The Germans are rumored to have left. Nobody knows anything. Crazy mood. Everybody's full of expectation. . . .

MAY 5, SATURDAY: *Schluss!* [The end!]

AFTERWORD

THE GERMANS LEFT Theresienstadt on May 5, 1945. Karel Kosvanec showed up unexpectedly and begged me to go home
with him because Theresienstadt was rampant with typhoid.
He sat me on his bicycle and took me to his house. That night
I woke up with a high temperature; I did not think I would survive the night. I asked Karel to take me back to the ghetto: I
knew I had typhoid and could be cared for in the ghetto hospital by the International Red Cross. I remember little of the
next six weeks, but when I was released, I had nowhere to go
and was utterly destitute—the few personal belongings left to
me had been stolen.

Then Otto's mother, who had helped to care for me while I
was hospitalized, received a letter from her only surviving son,
Evžen, saying that he had been returned to Prague from a concentration camp and was sharing an apartment with several
other survivors. For the next three months I lived in that
three-bedroom apartment with fifteen to twenty people, all of
whom subsisted on the food and clothing provided by the
local Jewish refugee organization. Leaving Theresienstadt
meant freedom for the first time in four years. I should have
been elated. I was not. I was deeply unhappy, emotionally
numb. Life seemed to have lost its meaning. I could not understand why I had survived. At first I hoped to find someone else
from my family, but after meeting people coming from Poland
and learning for the first time of the gas chambers and exter-

mination camps, I realized I was alone and would never see my family again.

Richard had non-Jewish relatives in Prague, but I could not remember their name, so I sat down with a phone book and started going through it from the letter *a*. I recognized the name when I came to it: Šindelář. I phoned them. Not only were they glad to hear I had come back, they told me that Richard had returned from England as a member of the Czech army. In fact, he had been in Prague a few days before for a victory celebration but had to leave because the Soviets refused to allow western soldiers to remain in Prague. He had tried to find his family and had written to Theresienstadt to inquire about them and me. But even though I was in the ghetto hospital at the time his letter arrived, the reply he received said that we had all been sent to Poland. The Šindelářs gave me his address and, wary of his feelings, I wrote him a cautious letter—after all, he could have married someone else by then. But I told him where he could reach me should he wish to. The day after he received the letter, he showed up at our apartment.

I cannot describe what I felt seeing him there in the doorway. It was a combination of joy and uncertainty. I had dreamt about that moment so many times, but when I actually saw him, I felt I no longer knew him. More than six years had passed. We had to get to know each other all over again. Since there could be no privacy in the crowded apartment, we took a long walk. Once Richard's three-day leave was up, he went back to his regiment; I stayed in Prague.

During the next few months Richard used his every leave to find a place for us to live. He was discharged in August 1945, and we were married three weeks later. We went to the cemetery for our honeymoon. It was our only way of visiting our families.

We did our best to lead a normal life again. We had a daughter in 1946 and a son four years later. We both worked as best we could during the ups and downs of the Communist regime, but Richard's service in the Czech army in England combined with the fact that we were Jewish and did not come from a working-class background caused years of fear, uncertainty, and professional persecution. Now life has come full circle. Richard died on January 7, 1993, fortunately having lived long enough to see his country return to democracy, his children grown and settled, and his four grandchildren healthy and happy. Through all our difficulties we never failed to appreciate having found each other and being given the chance to start a new family. We always relied on each other for understanding and support.

I continue to live in Prague near my son and his family, but I spend every summer in Ohio with my daughter and her family. Our parents would be happy to see us together.

EVA MÄNDLOVÁ ROUBÍČKOVÁ

TRANSLATOR'S NOTE

THERESIENSTADT, now called by its Czech name, Terezín, is located in the Czech Republic. It was built as a fortress in 1780 by the empress Maria Theresa of Austria, but from 1941 to 1945 it was used by the Nazis as a walled ghetto or concentration camp for Jews. The status of Theresienstadt was in flux from the very beginning. It was described as a ghetto, a concentration camp, a model camp used to impress foreign delegations, and finally as a transit station to the extermination camps. More than 155,000 human beings passed through Theresienstadt, of whom 35,000 perished, and 88,000 were sent to their deaths, mostly to Auschwitz in Poland. Neither Eva nor the other prisoners knew exactly how Theresienstadt differed from the other camps, or where the transports were destined, but terror of them stemmed from families being torn apart and, as Eva recalls, "a familiar evil was still better than the unknown."

The first two transports from Prague to Theresienstadt began in November and December of 1941. Over thirteen hundred able-bodied men between the ages of eighteen and forty and twenty-three staff members were sent to prepare the future ghetto for the massive deportation of Jews. This group of construction workers and administrators was known as the *Aufbaukommando* (AK). They later assumed leading positions in the "Jewish self-government," and their families were promised protection from Poland, had more food and better housing, and were given extra privileges. The *Ältestenrat* (Council of Elders) was the highest organ of the "Jewish self-government," but in reality, it served as the right hand for German officials, and its leaders were often considered even more brutal than the SS. The council was made up of various language and political groups, and each of the representatives was determined to protect the largest number of his members in Theresienstadt. The infighting this caused, and the necessary evil of having the right connections in order to survive, made an already difficult situation unbearable.

Eva often complains of the need for connections to survive in Theresienstadt, but she manages through hard work and much luck to overcome food shortages, transports, and abominable housing conditions. Being one of the first to arrive in Theresienstadt, she was given the advantageous job of working in the vegetable gardens. This made it possible for her to smuggle food to her family, and it also provided protection from transports. Eva attributes her "luck" to the fact that she was young, healthy, and hardworking, but there was another factor that made it possible for her to survive, and that was her fortuitous encounter with Karel Kosvanec, a railroad worker from Bohušovice. Karel, also referred to as the "Aryan," held a major position in a powerful underground smuggling network. He helped Eva immensely throughout her imprisonment in Theresienstadt.

The transports were systematic in the beginning, but toward the end they were increasingly chaotic. The process was always the same: selection lists were compiled, the names of the people were announced, and then they would report for registration. Those summoned had a specific amount of time, which could be a matter of days or hours, in which to be packed and ready to go. They would next go to a special barracks or distribution area (called the sluice), where people were housed and organized for the transport. The incessant moving described in Eva's diary revolved around the organization of these maneuvers. Normal transports were arranged by the *Kommandant* (commanding officer), who determined the number of people needed for a specific day. The first to go were always the *Weisungen*—people who had been arrested and released from jail. Their summons to a transport was mandatory, and unlike others, they could not appeal the order. The rest of the groups were chosen by a committee in the Magdeburg barracks, which served as both the central office and residence for the Jewish Council of Elders. During the selection process, factors such as a person's economic status, profession (working in the vegetable gardens meant protection), or family were considered.

Eva often mentions the lectures, concerts, and plays for which Theresienstadt was famed. The ghetto housed an unusually large population of prominent scientists, artists, and musicians, and the Nazis made full use of it for propaganda purposes. Lectures, a coffeehouse, a music pavilion, concerts, a theater, and a cabaret were tolerated by the Nazis to impress international organizations with how "well" they treated their prisoners.

Despite the fact that Theresienstadt was not an extermination camp, the reality of hunger and bestial living conditions proved deadly. The barracks were better than the crowded blockhouses in the other camps in that they were designed for large groups of people, but still dirt, disease, and cramped living spaces were inescapable. Though prisoners were initially allowed to have supplies and food sent to them, this soon degenerated into a means for the SS to confiscate their possessions. The black market and smuggling were the only way to avoid starvation from the minimal rations provided by the camp.

Eva's diary was written in several notebooks ("or whatever else I could find") in German shorthand. Ironically, the cover of one notepad bears the inscription "Whatever is written shall not be forgotten." Though all her possessions were stolen while she was in the hospital, her diary was not lost—it survived the war, endless relocations, and time. The inscription on the cover proved true: what Eva has written shall never be forgotten.

MAP OF THERESIENSTADT CAMP

1. Hannover barracks: a dormitory for working men
2. Bakery and central grocery store
3. Hamburg barracks: a dormitory for women. It was also the central place for dispatching transports, the so-called Šlojska, or sluice (transport distribution area)
4. *Bahnhofstrasse*: a part of the railroad tracks built to handle transports more quickly
5. Sudeten barracks: the first dormitory for working men
6. Head guards' quarters
7. Viktoria Hotel: a canteen and apartments for the members of the camp's SS-Kommandatur
8. Ústí barracks: a storage space for the clothes and luggage confiscated from prisoners
9. Dresden barracks: a women's dormitory. The camp's jail was in the cellar
10. Vrchlabí barracks: the central hospital
11. The disinfection station
12. Magdeburg barracks: a seat of the Jewish Council of Elders and the Jewish administration

NAMES
THAT APPEAR FREQUENTLY IN EVA'S DIARY

Richard Roubíček (Raubitschek)—Eva's fiancé, who escaped to England. He tried but failed to get Eva and their families permission to go to England with him.

Antonia Mändl ("Mommy")—Eva's mother.

Arnost Mändl ("Daddy")—Eva's father. Arnost Mändl was a World War I hero who received Austria's highest gold medal of honor for courage. He was a special case because of his medal and because he had tuberculosis. When the transports started, people believed that illness might be a reason for being exempt from deportation.

Marie Raubitschek ("Mama")—Richard's mother.

Lotte—Richard's sister. Her husband, Bedřich, was on business in Chile when the deportation of Jews started. He tried but failed to have his family released from Theresienstadt.

Gi—Eva's uncle on the maternal side. He lived with the Mändls before the war.

Tante Gretl and Tante Flora—cousins of Eva's mother.

Eva Glauber—Eva's closest friend in Prague.

Benny Grünberger—a close friend of Eva's, and Eva Glauber's boyfriend. His brother, Danny, and his family were all part of the Jewish community in Prague.

184 *Fredy Kantor*—an artist who became engaged to Eva Glauber after Benny was sent to Poland.

Zwi—a friend in Eva's circle of friends from Prague.

Eva Taussig—she worked with Eva in the camp gardens. The Taussigs were part of the Jewish community in Prague.

Jarka Pollak—a friend of both Evas. He suffered from depression, went insane in the camp, and tried to commit suicide. After a period in the camp asylum, he was sent to Poland.

Jirka Gans—Eva Taussig's boyfriend in the camp.

Egon Forscher—he lived in the pigpen on the outskirts of the camp and was therefore able to contact people on the outside. After the war he emigrated to Australia.

The Glasers—he lived in the same apartment house as the Mändls in Prague. Mrs. Glaser was not Jewish, so her family was exempt from the early deportations.

The Kohns—another "mixed marriage" family that lived in the same house as the Mändls in Prague. They, too, were exempt from the early transports.

Otto Mändl—a relative of the Mändls.

Grandmother Raubitschek and Grandma Gibian—Richard's grandmothers.

Karl Reiner—a well-known musician. As a child, he took piano lessons from Eva's mother.

Fredy Hirsch—a kind of spiritual leader in Theresienstadt   185
and part of Eva's group of friends in Prague.

FRIENDS FROM THERESIENSTADT:

Karel Kosvanec (*the "Aryan"*)—a railroad worker in Bohušovice. He is referred to in the diary as the "Aryan" and later as "Karel." Karel met Eva while she was watching the camp's sheep in the pasture, and he supported Eva throughout her internment. Karel had a major position in an illegal smuggling ring that acquired a great deal of power.

Tonda and Wilda Bischitzki—founders and leaders of the gardens. They were prisoners in the camp.

Löbl—one of the leaders of the underground smuggling network. He worked closely with Karel, and even though he was arrested and tortured, he never revealed Karel's name. His brothers were also involved in the group.

Otto Kellner—Eva's boyfriend in the camp. He wanted to marry her, but was sent to Poland. Eva continued to take care of Otto's mother after he left, and after the war Otto's mother took care of Eva while she was in the hospital.

■　　■　　■

Dr. Fantl—a physician in the camp. He and his mother were part of Löbl's underground smuggling operation.

Pacovsky—he made connections between Eva and Karel. When the war ended, he stole all her possessions, which included three thousand cigarettes that Karel had given her. This was considered a small fortune at the time.

186 *Margit*—she married Egon Forscher while in the camp. They separated after the war and he emigrated to Australia.

Doris Schimmerling—a younger friend of Eva's and considered the most beautiful girl in the camp.

Käthe—a good friend in the camp.

Pepík Reiner—one of the Jewish leaders of the field workers.

Kraus—a liaison between Karel and Eva. Not to be confused with:

Kraus—a Jewish engineer who owned a large farm where Eva and her crew worked under SS surveillance. He was in charge of the field workers, harvesting, and care of animals. He treated the workers badly.

Lederer—a Jewish administrator for the vegetable gardens.

THE JEWISH COUNCIL OF ELDERS:

Jakob Edelstein—the Jewish Elder.

Otto Zucker—Edelstein's deputy.

Mandler

Murmelstein

Fiedler

Epstein

Löwenstein

Weidmann

GERMAN AND CZECH OFFICIALS:

SS-Obersturmführer Dr. Siegfried Seidl—the commander of the camp.

Kurzawe—a German civilian responsible for the gardens.

Heindl—the SS in charge of agriculture.

Burger and Rahm—SS officials.

Janeček—the Czech chief of police. He interrogated Eva when she was sent to jail, and after the war she testified against him. He was condemned to death.

Hašek—a policeman also involved in Eva's interrogation.

Dr. Reinisch—the chief SS physician in the camp.

■   ■   ■

Aufbaukommando (*AK*)—the first group of workers who were transported to Theresienstadt to prepare the ghetto and barracks for the arrival of Jews. They were considered the founding members of Theresienstadt and became leaders in the "Jewish self-government." They and their families were promised protection from deportation to Poland, and enjoyed special privileges, such as more food and better housing.

Bohušovice—the town where the transports were sent initially.

The Crete (or *Kreta*)—a field where Eva worked outside the camp. It was near the crematorium.

Judenrein (or *Judenfrei*)—literally translated, "cleansed of Jews" or "free of Jews." It was the official Nazi terminology for a town from which all Jews had been deported.

Protectorate—the section of Czechoslovakia that was occupied by the Germans during World War II. The Protectorate ended at the border of Slovakia.

Schanzen—Theresienstadt was founded as a fortress more than two hundred years ago for Empress Maria Theresa. At that time, it had a moat and a wall surrounding it. The Schanzen are the moat and wall or a shack built into the wall for storage.

Sluice (*Schleusse*)—a word used in the camp to designate the barracks where people were assigned transports. Once a person was called, he or she would gather all his or her belongings and take them to the sluice, where they would reside until the transport was ready.

Weisung—an order for deportation to Poland that could not be appealed. Most people who were arrested for crimes in the camp were given this order. They would be called *Weisungen*.